W9-BRA-616

1974

AMERICAN WOMEN IN SPORTS

AMERICAN WOMEN IN SPORTS

BY PHYLLIS HOLLANDER

AN ASSOCIATED FEATURES BOOK

A W. W. NORTON BOOK

Published by

Grosset & Dunlap, Inc., New York

A National General Company

For Susan . . . a good sport always.

Library of Congress Catalog Card Number: 73-153920
ISBN 0-448-21412-1 (trade edition)
ISBN 0-448-26182-0 (library edition)

Printed in the United States of America

CONTENTS

ACKNOWLEDGMENTS

I have known women in sports all my life. From my earliest days, inspired by my active, always-on-the-go mother, I learned to be a doer and not a watcher. As a city child, generally confined to such street sports as stick-ball and roller skating, I found joy in the summers I spent at a utopian camp named Red Wing in the Adirondack Mountains. There I learned to appreciate not only the beauty of nature around me, but also the pleasures of such active sports as swimming, sailing, tennis and horseback riding.

I have been fortunate in having friends who also love sports—Belle Gersten, counselor; Shirley Burnett, physical education teacher; Nancy Lovitt, fellow schuss-boomer; Bunny Leyton, tennis partner; and Sig Wiener, sports researcher and fan.

I am appreciative of the assistance I have received from the various sports specialists who supplied some of the material and perspectives needed for this book: Bob Paul of the U.S. Olympic Committee; Ruth Jones of the Ladies' Professional Golf Association; Matt Merola of AMF Bowling; Arthur Serbo of the Brunswick Corporation; Norma Kirkendall of the Women's International Bowling Congress; equestrian writer George Coleman and the late Jack Zanger, sportswriter. I also thank Dorothy Bebon, typist.

There have been two editors in my life—my editor-father, Harry Rosen, who read copy on me until I married, and my husband Zander, sportswriter and editor, who patiently and painfully helped me give birth to a book.

PHOTO CREDITS

The author and publisher wish to thank the following sources for making their photos available to us:

United Press International: 7; 18; 26; 33; 45, bottom; 58, top; 63; 68, top; 68, bottom; 81, bottom; 87, top; 100, top; 106, bottom

Wide World Photos: 30; 38; 45, top; 49; 58, bottom; 68, left; 81, top; 87, center; 87, bottom; 94; 100, bottom

New York Racing Association (Bob Coglianese): 11

Brunswick Corporation: 106, top

AMERICAN WOMEN IN SPORTS

Introduction

A VERY LONG time ago, in ancient Greece, women were barred not only from participation in the Olympic games, but they were also forbidden to watch them. When Pherenice, a widow of noble birth, sneaked into the games to watch her son race, she was discovered by the guards, arrested, found guilty, and sentenced to death.

Such harsh and unjust discrimination caused a wealthy noblewoman named Hippodamia to establish a sporting festival for women only, known as the Herea.

Since that time, sports-minded women everywhere have continued the struggle for recognition as athletes. It was not until 1900, however, that any special events for women were included in the modern Olympic games.

Here in America, the story of women's fight for acceptance on the athletic field is an inspiring one. The tremendous effort, sacrifice, and skill needed to make any champion is a vital part of the story, but the particular obstacles confronting the so-called weaker sex are at the heart of this book.

In colonial days, women were considered an economic necessity in the home. Who would bake the bread, weave the cloth, sew the clothes, and draw the water from the well if mother and her daughters were out swimming in John Smith's creek or playing ten pins on the village green? So although women were not actually barred from recreational sports, there just was no time to indulge in them. And certainly the Puritans would have frowned upon such frolicking.

In the years following the industrial revolution, the work load was lessened. There were sewing machines, mechanical looms, and running water in the house to free women from their home-bound chores. But American women now had another problem. What would the neighbors think? For no self-respecting young lady of the times would be seen in public heartily swinging a golf club in a mini-skirt or diligently pumping the high diving board in a skintight bikini. These women lived in a prudish, restricting society, where they were presumed to be weak and soft and expected to be covered up. Certainly they were not suited for the rigorous training required to make a champion.

So it took an extraordinary female to turn her back on society and set out on a road formerly reserved for men only. She had to be courageous, physically fit, and full of the same zeal and stick-to-it-iveness that had produced our male athletes.

Fortunately for American women there were such crusaders: women like Eleanora Sears, a society girl from Boston; Gertrude Ederle, who swam the English Channel; Helen Wills, tennis queen; and the incomparable Babe Didrikson. Some of these old-timers were shining stars too long ago to be remembered, but some were of such magnitude that they will live forever. They were the trailblazers. They were the first women to shed the heavy serge bloomers and long skirts and appear in public ready for action sports—in tank suits, riding jodhpurs, and shorts.

Today, sports are virtually a part of every girl's growing-up, in school and out. With the growth of recreational facilities and leisure time, hundreds of thousands of women and girls are participating in almost every sport open to men, including such uncommon and spectacular ones as horseracing, skydiving, surfing, and bullfighting.

The stories in this book are of the heroines of today and yesterday who rose to fame in those sports most commonly enjoyed by girls today—on a horse, golf course, tennis court, bowling lane, and cinder track, as well as on the water, ice, and snow.

The tales told here are for every girl to dream on, sportsminded or not. For these are the adventures of every girl, short and tall, old and young, married and single, rich and poor, feminine and tomboyish.

You will certainly find your idol here. If she is not one of the emancipators of days long past, then she will be one of the lovely, spirited, self-disciplined young athletes of today.

CHAPTER 1

Pioneers
on
Horseback

THE FIFTH AVENUE strollers clutched their coats
tightly about them in the chill of the January air. Suddenly
the normal street noises of this day in 1912 were inter-
rupted by the sound of clattering hoof beats. Looking
toward the street, the startled pedestrians watched a
coach with four galloping horses thunder down the avenue.

Seated high in the coachman's seat, expertly clutching
the reins in white-gloved hands, was a thirty-one-year-old
woman—head held boldly, eyes flashing with the pleasure
and excitement of the ride. Miss Eleanora Sears, in re-
sponse to a sporting wager, was once again shocking
American society by appearing in public in a traditionally
male role—this time driving a four-in-hand like a professional coachman.

Eleo, the blonde, blue-eyed darling of high Boston society, was a great-great-granddaughter of Thomas Jefferson
and the daughter of Frederick Sears, a wealthy shipping

and real estate tycoon. As such, she was expected to conform to the conventions and proprieties of her time and position. Proper young ladies were saddled in the drawing rooms, sipping tea, not high in the saddle of galloping mares.

High-spirited Eleanora, born into sedate society in 1881, was not content with a gentle game of croquet now and then. By the time she was in her teens she had begun her pilgrimage into the all-male world of sports, looking for excitement, competition, and perfection with the skill and persistence of any male athlete.

At night, elegantly gowned, she followed the social set from Boston to Newport, Rhode Island, from New York to Southampton, Long Island, dancing and frolicking with wealthy and titled young men until the wee hours of the morning. But with the coming of daylight, she occupied herself with the forbidden pursuit of outdoor sports.

Eleanora's range of activities was incredible in those days, and even today. She was a whiz at tennis, drove a golf ball 200 yards, played polo like a cavalryman, and swam with the fishes. She tried anything on a dare and was among the first women to race a car and fly an airplane. She was the first of her sex to swim the 4½ miles from Bailey's Beach to First Beach along the elegant Newport shore. Even at such sports as hunting, fishing, and canoeing, she was an expert.

In 1910 a national magazine described Miss Sears as "the best all-around athlete in American society." Yet, society did not praise Eleanora. It chastised her. When she appeared on an all-male polo field in 1912 wearing breeches instead of the traditional long skirt, and riding astride a pony instead of sidesaddle, a hue and cry arose. The Mothers' Club of Burlingham, California, angrily passed a public resolution denouncing her appearance:

Such unconventional trousers and clothes of the masculine sex are contrary to the hard and fast customs of our ancestors. It is immodest and wholly unbecoming a woman, having a bad effect on the sensibilities of our boys and girls.

They demanded that Miss Sears "restrict herself to the

usual feminine attire in the future." There followed, too, in other parts of the country, many a sermon preached against her wickedness.

But Eleo, who had already been voted to society's "best-dressed list," was not to be restricted in her sporting costumes. Competition was the spice in her life and she continued to wear whatever she thought appropriate for comfort in sport. She adopted "shocking" outfits for swimming, sailing, figure skating, and tennis.

In her comfortable attire she became a champion at competitive tennis and squash. In tennis, she won the national doubles title four times, mixed doubles once, and was a finalist in the singles twice. In squash, she was captain of the International Squash Racquets team, president of the Women's Squash Association, as well as the first national titleholder in 1928. In 1954, when she was seventy years young, she was still competing in the national squash championships.

When Eleo was in her forties, she took up her most attention-getting activity—long-distance walking. She made the headlines as a result of her annual 47-mile walk from Providence to Boston. Her fast-paced record for this stroll was 9 hours 53 minutes. She also walked 73 miles from Newport to Boston in 17 hours. Even when Eleo was in Europe, she went strolling. Once, when visiting France, she walked the 42½ miles from Fontainebleau to the Ritz Bar in Paris in 8½ hours.

Yet despite Miss Sears' myriad activities, it was her preoccupation with horses that dominated her life. She was a superb horsewoman, riding in the steeplechase at horse shows and hunt meets. In later years, she devoted her time to raising championship horses, for show as well as for racing. During most of her adult life she found time to ride at least four hours every day.

And as Eleanora Sears started out making news with horses, so she was to finish. In November 1967, the *New York Post* carried a feature story about Eleo:

. . . the regal, white-haired woman who sits in Box 72 [at the National Horse Show in Madison Square Garden] *each night is Miss Eleanora Sears of Pride's Crossing, Massachu-*

Fast-paced Eleanora Sears is on one of her 47-mile walks from Providence, Rhode Island to Boston, Massachusetts.

Olympic equestrian Kathy Kusner, the beautiful horsewoman whose court battle to obtain a Maryland jockey license ended in victory, was a winner on show horses.

setts. She has had horses at the Garden every year since the National has been held. . . . This year she has two hunters in the show. Miss Sears has also loaned horses to the U.S. Equestrian team ever since it was founded. . . . Leafing back through 41 years of Garden programs, it is hard to find a show when a Sears horse didn't win blue ribbons. For many years, too, she rode them herself.

But Eleanora would ride no more. She died in 1968 at the age of eighty-seven, gallant and energetic till the end.

More than half a century after Miss Sears thundered down Fifth Avenue, another female pioneer on horseback was to make the news. On October 22, 1968, Kathy Kusner, one of this country's leading Olympic riders, was granted a jockey's license by the Maryland Racing Commission. Until that time, women had not been permitted to ride on the thoroughbred racetracks of America. Kathy's historic victory for the equality of her sex had been preceded, however, by her long list of other victories as a horseback rider.

From the time Kathy joined the U.S. Olympic team in 1961, she had been a leading American rider. She had competed in every recognized horse show in the world, winning most of the major prizes. She won the President's Cup in Washington, the New York championships in Madison Square Garden, the Prix des Amazones in Rotterdam, Holland, and the Irish Trophy in Dublin, Ireland, among others.

Kathy, who was born in 1940, was raised in the fox-hunting states of Virginia and Maryland. When she was ten, she had her own pony, which she kept in the backyard of her home in Arlington, Virginia. She cleaned out stables and groomed horses to earn board for her pony. Her father, a government mathematician, had little knowledge or interest in horses, but he did believe that his daughter should do whatever interested her.

Kathy was soon taking riding lessons and entering show and ring events. During her teens at Washington and Lee High School, she showed horses for dealers in Virginia and continued to ride, groom, and train whenever and wherever possible.

Her love for horses was all-consuming. "I want to ride forever," she said. She liked horses better than people and once commented to her father, "Wouldn't the world be a lot simpler if it were full of horses?"

When she was eighteen, Kathy set a women's horse-jump record (7 feet 3 inches), and in 1961 she became the first woman in ten years to join the U.S. equestrian team. She rode on the U.S. gold medal team in the Pan-American games in 1963 and again in the 1964 Olympics. In 1966, during a European tour, she won the International Grand Prix at Dublin as well as six other major European classes. She had taken the Dublin prize the year before and thus became the only rider in history to win this event twice in a row on the same horse, a spirited steed named Untouchable.

By 1967, Kathy had earned the reputation of leading lady equestrian in the world. She was 103 pounds of champion in the only Olympic sport where men and women compete against each other. That year, the U.S. team consisted of seven members, four of whom were women. At the National Horse Show in Madison Square Garden, Kathy rode off with a major share of the honors, besting topflight riders from all over the world.

Yet, in spite of all Kathy's achievements, she still held on to what seemed to be an impossible dream. She wanted to be a jockey.

In November 1967, she applied for a jockey license with the Maryland Racing Commission. Although in 1943 Judy Johnson had been granted a license to ride in the steeplechase at the Pimlico (Maryland) track, no woman had yet been licensed to ride in the flat racing events. With the passage of a stronger Civil Rights Act in 1964 forbidding discrimination in employment because of sex, race, national origin, or religion, Kathy believed she had a good case. The Commission turned her down, but fortunately for the members of her sex, Kathy was not sidetracked from her purpose.

"Horse-riding is more a game of technique and skill

than strength," she said. "It's the same as playing chess with men, so I don't intend to give up the fight."

After a year of court battles, Kathy's perseverance was rewarded. Judge Ernest A. Loveless overturned the Commission's ruling. "This court," stated the judge, "finds that no reasonable mind could possibly have reached the factual conclusion that the Maryland Commission did." The judge ordered a reversal on the grounds that Kathy's license had been refused on the basis of sex discrimination.

Following along the same legal lines, the Kentucky Racing Commission granted a license to Penny Ann Early, a twenty-five-year-old mother. Now the race was on to see who would actually be entered competitively and thus claim the official title as "first lady jockey." Unfortunately neither girl made it. Penny Ann encountered a boycott by male jockeys at Churchill Downs and Kathy, the Olympian who started it all, was sidelined with a broken leg.

But the starting gates were now open to women, and the list of firsts began to mount along with additional lady jockeys. Diane Crump led the pack when she became the first woman to race against men on a flat pari-mutuel track (February 8, 1969, at Hialeah in Florida). Soon "jockette" became a familiar expression on the sport pages of the nation's newspapers. By the end of 1969 more than twenty women had acquired that designation.

Pert, pigtailed Barbara Jo Rubin became the first woman to win a thoroughbred race (February 22, 1969, in Charlestown, West Virginia). Barbara Jo was subsequently forced to retire because of torn knee cartilage, but not before she had ridden in 89 races which included 22 victories and a historic female debut at New York's famed Aqueduct track.

But it was Diane Crump who claimed perhaps the most significant "first" when, on May 2, 1970, she broke the sex barrier at the ninety-six-year-old Kentucky Derby, racing's most hallowed event. No greenhorn on the tracks, this professional jockey had won 33 races against men during the year and a half before her Derby ride. Although Diane placed 15th in the 17-horse field, what mattered was that now the barriers were all down.

Barbara Jo Rubin was the first woman jockey to ride at New York's famed Aqueduct racetrack—in March, 1969.

Whether in the coachman's seat, or as an Olympic equestrian, whether holding the reins in a sulky or astride a thoroughbred racer, American women had proved they could ride with or against any man.

CHAPTER 2

Swimming the Channel

THE TUG BOAT *Macom* moved slowly up the bay and into New York Harbor. Every steamship within range had tied down its whistle-cord in open position, sirens from small craft close by blasted forth in one continuous wail, and overhead, airplanes swooped low in salute while dropping flowers on the deck of the tug.

Standing at the bow, surrounded by masses of crushed petals, reporters, and city dignitaries in frock coats and striped trousers, was an apple-cheeked, cherubic-looking girl of nineteen.

At the Battery, the passengers disembarked and were loaded into open-topped limousines for the ride up lower Broadway to City Hall where Jimmy Walker, Mayor of New York City, waited. Broadway was unrecognizable. On this hot August day in 1926, the ground was covered with a blanket of white. This was no freak snow storm, but the litter from torn-up telephone books, shredded newspapers, and ticker tape cascading down from the office windows lining the streets.

The crowds on the sidewalks were spilling over the curb and into the street, giving the motorcade barely enough room to move. Never before had there been such a tumultuous welcome in the streets of New York.

The young girl, now sitting next to Grover Whalen, the city's official greeter, stood up in the open car and reached out her arms as if to embrace the crowd. For this giant display of affection was for her, Gertrude "Trudy" Ederle, daughter of a New York City shopkeeper, who on August 6 had been the first woman to swim the twenty miles across the English Channel—and in the record-breaking time of 14 hours 31 minutes!

Until that day in August, only five men had succeeded in conquering the Channel, and the record time had stood at a little over 16½ hours set by an Argentine, Enrique Tiraboschi. Now the world had another record-holder and it was a woman, no more than 5 feet 5 inches tall.

Trudy was overwhelmed at the reception, so different from her return to New York the year before. Then she was just another of the many defeated Channel swimmers. Today she was a heroine and she remembered with pride the events of that historic August 6 swim.

It had been a cold, damp morning, for the sun had not yet risen. The sea was calm, however, and the weather forecast, as predictable as it could be in those days, was good. The announcement was made. Trudy would go. The icy, menacing waters of the English Channel stretched out before her.

Excitedly, she pulled on her red jersey one-piece bathing suit and prepared for the ordeal ahead. After being smeared all over with nearly six pounds of thick black grease to protect her from the cold, she adjusted her bathing cap and pulled her goggles down over her eyes. At 7:08 French summer time she waded out into the sea at Cape Gris-Nez, France.

Following closely alongside was the French tug *Alsace,* with the words "This Way Ole Kid" and an arrow pointing forward painted on her leeward side. On board were Trudy's trainer, Thomas Burgess, her father, Henry, and sister, Margaret, and swimmers, Louis Timson of England, Ishak Helmy of Egypt, and Lillian Cannon from Baltimore.

For the first lap of the trip, the weather and sea conditions were good and Trudy was able to cover four miles in less than three hours. At about 10:30 in the morning she had her first meal, some beef extract, while floating on her back. Those on board wrote some of the cheering messages wired to the tug from America on a blackboard which they lowered over the side for her to read.

At varying intervals, the swimmers aboard the tug would dive into the sea and encourage Trudy with their fresh, strong strokes. Miss Cannon swam with her for about an hour during which time Trudy had a second meal of hot chocolate, which she offered to share with her friend swimming alongside.

But the conditions changed. At 1:30 in the afternoon, only nine miles from the English coast, it started to rain and the going got rough. The winds were blowing fiercely and the temperature had begun to drop rapidly. The alongside-swimmers were returning from their short swims exhausted and nauseous from the pounding seas.

To offer encouragement to Trudy, the party aboard the tug was singing loudly, "Yes, We Have No Bananas" and other pop tunes of the day. Newsmen and photographers on another accompanying boat turned up the volume on the victrola so Trudy could hear her favorite song, "Let Me Call You Sweetheart." But the winds began to drown out the sounds. By 5:00 the waves were of such ominous proportions that Thomas Burgess began to worry about Trudy's safety. He knew well what this young girl was going through, for he had tried 19 times before becoming the second person to beat the Channel in 1911.

At twilight, after having been in the water for 12 hours, fighting a rough sea, a tide running against her, and stinging salt spray battering her face, it seemed as if Trudy would have to give up.

Burgess no longer felt he could be responsible for what might happen. He yelled over the side of the wallowing tug. "Trudy, you must come out!" But the indomitable Trudy, with her legs never missing a beat in their six-beat crawl, shouted back, "What for?" and on she swam.

Darkness had fallen. The coast of England from Deal to South Foreland was now aglow with red, green, and blue flares. Crowds had massed on the beach, all eyes scanning the dark and murky waters for some sign of the approaching swimmer. At exactly 9:39, 14 hours 31 minutes after starting out, Gertrude Ederle waded out of the water at Kingsdown, England. This shy, retiring nineteen-year-old girl had become the first woman to swim the English Channel and in doing it she had beaten a man's record!

In record-breaking time, too, all of America would be reading the story and looking at the picture of their greased and goggled heroine. Captain Patterson, publisher of the *Chicago Tribune* and the *New York Daily News,* had backed Trudy with the money needed to make this attack on the Channel. Now, he had his story. He set up a spectacular relay system in order to get word of Trudy's triumph to his readers first. The news copy and pictures were placed in a waterproof casing and put on an Empress steamer of the Canadian Pacific line whose destination was Montreal. When it reached the edge of North America, it was dropped into the ocean, picked up by a seaplane, transferred to a land plane, tossed into a racing car piloted by a famous racing driver, and through the fog and rain of the night traveled by railroad and finally ambulance to the *Daily News* offices in New York City. It was a scoop, received 12 hours before any other paper in the United States.

And so, on the morning of August 7, 1926, all of America was reading about Gertrude Ederle. Now, several weeks later, all of New York City was out to praise her. This quiet young girl living over her father's delicatessen on Amsterdam Avenue in New York City could hardly believe that all this fuss and tumult was in her honor.

Trudy was a humble girl whose wholesomeness and sweetness of disposition were reflected on her face. When she was thirteen, she had joined the Women's Swimming

Association, a swim club on the lower east side of Manhattan. For a youngster surrounded by the usual soot and cement of a big city, it was a real joy to escape to the cool refreshing waters of the club pool. Her joy soon became a passion and in less than a year she had begun to show the makings of a champion swimmer. In the international 3-mile swim for the J. P. Day Cup in 1921, she earned her first record. Swimming in that New York Bay race, she defeated more than 50 of the world's outstanding swimmers. And this was the first time she had ever competed in a race over 220 yards.

Spurred on by the victory, Trudy began to spend long hours working out at the pool. The Women's Swimming Association had been founded in 1917 by a group of secretaries and business women. By the time Trudy had joined the club, such women as Claire Galligan and Charlotte Boyle (exponents of the then new American crawl) and Ethel McGary, a national long-distance champion, were famous club members. During the next few years, Trudy joined their ranks by breaking world standards for every race from 100 to 800 meters.

By 1924, when she was only seventeen years old, she held 18 world's distance records. At the Olympic games in Paris that year, Trudy won a gold medal as a member of the championship U.S. 400-meter relay team and two bronze medals for her third places in the 100- and 400-meter freestyle races.

In spite of all of these victories, her coach (and the coach of many other Olympic swimmers), L. de B. Handley, was troubled by a failing in Trudy's personality. She lacked confidence and became very easily discouraged. "If it hadn't been for her older sister, Margaret," he said, "Trudy might have given up. Margaret, whom she worshipped, coaxed and encouraged, scolded and bullied, as circumstances prompted, always getting results." For example, once when Gertrude was almost within reach of a record-breaking swim from the Battery to Sandy Hook, she began to slow down. Margaret shouted from the accompanying boat, "Get going lazy bones, you're loafing."

Florence Chadwick proved that a determined and dedicated woman athlete could have the strength and endurance of a man.

Gertrude Ederle, the first woman to swim across the English Channel, acknowledges the cheering crowds in the New York City ticker tape parade honoring her in August, 1926.

"Loafing, am I?" puffed back the exhausted Trudy. "For that I'll make it if it kills me."

And make it she did—for her sister Margaret, herself, and as history proved in 1926, for all the women of America.

A month after she became the first woman to swim the English Channel, an editorial appeared in the *Saturday Evening Post.* "Her [Gertrude Ederle's] youth and gay courage captured the imagination of all continents. . . . In all the annals of sport there is no finer record than that rung up by this young American girl. . . . There is every reason to hope and believe that Miss Ederle's great achievement will intensify interest in swimming as a sport for both men and women."

Until that time, swimming as a competitive sport was still for the relatively few. Women, so long bogged down by heavy woolen bloomers and long-sleeved jerseys were just emerging from the dunking stage. With Trudy's triumph, people began to realize what advantages could be derived from swimming.

"Protection from drowning is not the only immunity the frequent swimmer enjoys. Swimming not only enlarges the lung capacity and develops wind and muscle, but it also builds up a stubborn resistance to disease," said one leading publication of the time. One writer pointed out that Gertrude Ederle had lost 12 pounds during her famous swim and dispelled the common misconception of the time that one had to be overly padded with fat in order to excel as a swimmer.

Helen Wainwright, a champion swimmer in the early 1900s, was prompted by Trudy's triumph to point out that in competitive marathon swimming women actually had an advantage over men. "We can surpass the proud male," she said. "In swimming over a period of 6 to 12 hours, a woman can cover greater distances than a man. Her bones are smaller, body lighter. Her frame is more generously covered with flesh and therefore more buoyant."

Miss Wainwright's observations were borne out in the

years that followed. In fact, the same year that Gertrude Ederle made her record-breaking swim, a child of ten made her first distance swim across the channel at the mouth of San Diego Bay in California. And thus another American girl started on her way to a first in long-distance swimming.

The youngster, Florence Chadwick, daughter of a detective and narcotics agent with the San Diego Police Department, showed early signs of becoming a champion. Swimming in her first race in a local pool when she was only six, she went on to become winner of the annual 2½-mile race at La Jolla, California, ten times.

Miss Chadwick discovered early that her successes came only in the long-distance swims. Freestyle short sprints were not her speed, so Florence's attentions turned toward a long-distance goal. It was also a goal that would require much money, and Florence knew that her education would be an important means to this end. So she concentrated hard on her studies.

While at school, she found time to be on the swimming team at Point Loma High and a member of the Girl Reserves. Before her graduation, she became president of the student government.

Not satisfied to end her formal education yet, Florence spent a year at San Diego State College and attended a business school before finally training at the comptometer school of the Felt and Tarrant Manufacturing Company.

In 1948, after saving enough money from her work in a movie with swimming star Esther Williams and as a swim instructor at the La Jolla Beach and Tennis Club, she was ready for the first lap of her journey toward that long-distant goal. She left her home in California to take a job as a comptometer operator in the offices of the Arabian-American Oil Company in far-off Saudi Arabia.

Her swim training regimen began in the 150-foot pool near her office. Later, she was transferred to an office in Ras Al Mishah near the rough and treacherous Persian Gulf. This was just the opportunity she was looking for, and her training continued in the icy waters of the Gulf. Before and after work, sometimes well into the night,

Florence swam. Often, after a hard day at the office, she would spend as much as ten hours in the water, before falling exhaustedly into bed.

At last she was ready for the first lap of her goal, the swim across the English Channel. On a relatively calm day in June 1950, Florence Chadwick swam the Channel from France to England. As a matter of fact, she beat Gertrude Ederle's time by one hour 11 minutes. But Florence's goal was still to be reached.

Swimming the Channel from France to England had by this time become fairly commonplace. What Florence Chadwick had been training for, however, was to swim back in the other direction, from England to France, against the tides and winds. It was a task so formidable that no woman had ever achieved it.

The following year she was back in England. For weeks she waited in a Dover hotel for favorable weather and sea conditions. She tried to put on some weight by eating starches and ice cream. She averaged about three or four hours in the water daily and went to bed by 9:30 every night with the hope that the next day might be right for her reverse attack on the Channel.

Finally, on an August morning in a soupy fog, with unfavorable tides and waves heavily tipped with white-caps, Florence, now past thirty, got tired of waiting.

The water was icy cold and rough. Soon she was suffering from severe nausea and her trainer gave her seasickness pills to help. The sickness passed, but now she had another more formidable foe—the terrible cold. The coat of protective grease on her body had washed off and her arms and legs were numb. The fog was so thick now that she couldn't even see the boat cruising alongside her. Every stroke was an agony and she had slowed down almost to treading water. But still she struggled on.

At last, 16 hours 22 minutes after starting out, Florence dragged herself ashore. With her hands and body cut and bruised from the off-shore rocks, she shook hands with the mayor of Sangatte, France.

And so Florence Chadwick had achieved her goal. At thirty-three years of age, she had become the first woman

in the world to swim the English Channel in both direc-
tions!

CHAPTER 3

Faster,
Farther,
Higher

"ON YOUR MARK, get set—go!" The starter's gun re-sounded through the Olympic stadium and the runners were off. Trailing a little behind the pack on this stifling September day in Rome, 1960, was a 5-foot, 11-inch, 132-pound Afro-American girl—long, lean, and graceful as a deer in flight.

Twenty-year-old Wilma Rudolph was striding longer and faster now. The gap between the lead runner, Russia's Maria Itkina, was closing. At the halfway mark, 50 meters, Wilma forged ahead. Eleven seconds after the crack of the starter's gun, Wilma Rudolph snapped the finish-line tape, three yards ahead of her nearest competitor. She had won the 100-meter dash, and her first Olympic gold medal.

This was only the beginning of Wilma's race to fame. In the days that followed, this lovely young girl with the sleekness and grace of a panther ran off with two more gold medals. In the 200-meter dash she broke the Olympic record and in the team event, the 400-meter relay, she and her teammates set a world and Olympic mark. She was the first American woman athlete to win three gold medals in Olympic track and field.

Sixteen years earlier, when Wilma was a child in Clarksville, Tennessee, she had been unable to walk. After a siege of double pneumonia and scarlet fever, one leg had been left completely useless. Her mother, who had borne nineteen children, carried Wilma for weekly visits to a clinic in Nashville. There Wilma received heat and water therapy to revive her shrunken muscles. At home, Wilma's brothers and sisters took turns massaging her legs.

For over two years, the child was confined to a chair or bed. All during those painful, unhappy days, Wilma never complained. "It didn't make her cross," her mother said. "The other children came and played with her while she sat in her chair."

At last when she was about six, with the help of specially made shoes, Wilma started to walk again. It didn't take her long to make up for those long years of immobility. She was soon playing basketball and running races as well as any of her most active friends.

When she was thirteen, she made the Clarksville High basketball team. During practice one day she dribbled the ball wildly down the court and fell in an ungraceful heap at the feet of her coach, Clinton Gray. "A 'skeeter," he said. "You buzz around like a regular mosquito—fast, little, and always in my way."

But 'Skeeter was not little or in her coach's way for long. At fifteen, she had already grown to her full height, and was an all-state basketball player, scoring a school record of 803 points in 25 games. The track coach at Tennessee A & I State University, Ed Temple, recognized Wilma's potential as a runner. He encouraged Coach Gray to start a track team at Clarksville High so she could get the training and experience she needed.

In less than a year of high school competition, Wilma earned a berth on the U.S. Olympic team. In 1956, when she was sixteen years old, she went to Melbourne, Australia, for the Olympic games and helped the U.S. women's team win a bronze medal in the 400-meter relays.

Wilma returned home and enrolled at Tennessee A & I. There, her track training was intensified under the expert guidance of Coach Temple. His biggest concern was that skinny Wilma didn't eat enough to sustain her during the rigorous training program. "She won't eat and when she does, it's junk—hamburgers and pop," he complained.

She also liked her sleep and was often late for practice. In desperation, the coach ruled that all latecomers would have to run an extra lap for every minute they were tardy. Wilma was cured the hard way the following morning when she was half an hour late. She had to run the extra 30 laps. One of her teammates, Martha Hudson, said of her, "I guess Wilma would rather sleep than do most anything. Next to that it's reading, but mostly in bed."

It's certain, however, from her record, that sleep did not slow down Wilma Rudolph. Spurred on by a superior group of teammates at Tennessee A & I, Wilma's speed earned her the reputation of "America's fastest woman."

"She's great," said her coach, "but she couldn't have done it alone. Her teammates are the next three fastest girls in the country. Barbara Jones ran a world record 10.3 seconds for 100 yards at Randalls Island, New York, in 1958. Lucinda Williams and Martha Hudson also gave her a run for her money. Rudolph runs so fast because she is pressed so hard in practice. Without it, she wouldn't be nearly as good as she is."

This unusual team won six gold medals among them in the 1960 Olympics. After the games, Coach Temple (who was also an Olympic track coach) took his girls on tour, where they raced on tracks all over the world—in Athens, Amsterdam, London, Cologne, and Berlin. Wherever they went, the crowds besieged them.

Wilma was a cheerful heroine, beloved by everyone. In France they called her *La Perle Noire* (The Black Pearl); in Italy, *La Gazelle Nera* (The Black Gazelle). Back home in America, she was still known as 'Skeeter—the darting, buzzing, wisp of a mosquito, the only American to win

Wilma Rudolph, the only American athlete to place first in three track and field events in the same Olympic games, displays her three gold medals.

In 1930, nineteen-year-old Stella Walsh started on a running career that would bring her 40 U.S. championships during nearly a quarter of a century of competition.

three gold medals in track and field in the same Olympic games.

In a crowning tribute to Wilma, the Amateur Athletic Union in 1961 awarded her the Sullivan Memorial Trophy for her outstanding performance as an amateur athlete. Only two other women before her in the more than 25-year history of the trophy had received this treasured prize. The inscription on the trophy reads: "To the athlete, male or female, who by performance, example and good influence did the most to advance the cause of good sportsmanship."

Later that year, Wilma received an invitation to race in the usually all-male Millrose games held annually in Madison Square Garden, New York. Thirty-one years earlier, in 1930, another woman had been invited to race in this same event.

Stella Walsh, a nineteen-year-old sprinter from Cleveland, stunned 16,000 fans at the Garden by running the 50-yard dash in a world-record-breaking time of 6.1 seconds. Stella was named the "outstanding performer" of the meet, a distinction which had never gone to a woman before—or for that matter, since.

Stella Walsh was born Stanislawa Walasiewicz in Poland in 1911. She came to this country in her mother's arms when she was ten months old. "Since then I have been running in the streets, playgrounds, and high school gymnasiums," she said. "I don't think I ever walked."

Stella was raised in an athletic family. Her mother and her maternal grandfather loved sports and encouraged her to be active. On a visit back to Poland when she was in her teens, her grandfather, then seventy years old, challenged his "whippersnapper" granddaughter to a race around the family farm. "He really showed me a thing or two," Stella recalled, admiring his stamina.

Following her success in the Millrose games, Stella went on to become U.S. outdoor champion in the 100-meter dash (four times), the 200-meter dash (11 times), the broad jump (ten times) and indoor champion at 220 yards (six times) and 50 yards (twice). All told, she won 40 U.S.

championships and an Olympic gold medal for Poland in the 1932 Olympics at Los Angeles when she was not yet an American citizen. Her gold medal performance was a world record 11.9 clocking in the 100-meter dash. Sports writers claimed she had the nearest thing to a man's steady stride they had ever seen.

But it wasn't her collection of records and medals alone that made Stella Walsh one of America's greatest women athletes. It was her ability to sustain her racing skills over a long period of time. Stella won her first U.S. championship in 1930 (100-meter dash) when she was nineteen, and 18 years later she won that same championship for the fourth time. In 1953, 23 years after her first victory, she was still in major competition. At forty-two years of age, she entered the western regional meet of the Women's National AAU pentathlon championship. She won the five-event competition with a record-breaking performance.

Stanislawa Walasiewicz at forty-plus had turned back the clock and added another milestone to the growing accomplishments of this nation's women athletes.

Stella was not the only foreign-born athlete of whom America could be proud. Olga Fikotova of Czechoslovakia added still another dimension to our sporting landscape.

In the 1956 Olympics, Olga was competing for her native land in the discus throw. Exerting all her strength, she hurled the 2½-pound disc 176 feet 1½ inches for a gold medal. This mighty heave was 7 feet 5 inches more than the winning throw in the 1952 games. For her victory the Czech government named Olga "supreme master of sports"—the highest honor a Czech athlete can attain.

She became a national celebrity. For several years prior to the Olympic games, Olga had been breaking her country's records before as many as 30,000 spectators. Although she was a medical student at Charles University in Prague, she found time for the rigorous training required of a star athlete. A career in sports was a popular and much respected way of life for a Czechoslovakian woman.

With a gold medal around her neck, Olga looked forward to many more years as a national heroine.

But before the Olympic games were over, Olga's plans were to change dramatically. She met and fell in love with Harold Connolly, the American gold medalist in the 16-pound hammer throw. After several soul-searching months apart, Olga and Hal decided to get married, and Olga left her home and fans behind. Her new life in America would be with a man of a different background, education, and religion. She would be living in a Western democratic country, much opposed to the Communist government then in control of her native Czechoslovakia.

The wedding was heralded in a *New York Times* editorial on March 22, 1957. It read:

This poor old world of ours is quarreling, divided and perplexed. . . . The H-bomb overhangs us like a cloud of doom . . . but Olga and Harold are in love and the world does not say no to them. . . . Somehow this seems like a ray of light, intelligence and beauty in a world where ministers of state and heads of government go nervously back and forth in search of intelligence, light and beauty and do not often find them. There should be a little quiet dancing in the streets next Wednesday.

Olga found American attitudes toward women athletes very different from those of Europeans. In New England, where she and Harold set up their first home, she was amazed at the still prudish outlook toward women in competitive sport. Once, after encouraging a group of young girls at a high school assembly program to go out for sports, she was criticized by the school principal. "The hands of our girls are created to play violin," he said. "Please do not put ideas in their heads about competition."

Olga answered angrily, "For seven years I played the violin and my hands were as good for it as for winning the Olympic games."

It didn't take the new Mrs. Connolly long to realize that she would have a hard time getting to the top in American competition. In addition to keeping house for her school-teacher husband and caring for their infant son, Olga

*Olga Connolly, Olympic
discus champion, with her
husband Harold, Olympic
hammer champion, and the
first of their four sons.*

tried to continue her medical studies and work part-time in a medical laboratory. The tasks of finding high level competition and time for training were enormous.

"The meets in the United States are organized in deep seclusion and are very scarce," she complained. "The schools are making every effort to keep hard exercise and competition out of the curriculums. They want to keep American women feminine, they say."

In spite of all this, however, Olga, after first becoming a naturalized citizen, made the U.S. Olympic team in 1960, 1964, and 1968. By the time she and Harold went to Mexico City in 1968, they were the parents of four children.

Olga was pleasantly surprised by the success of the American women runners. Nonetheless, she still felt that America was weak in track and field promotion. "Unfortunately, Tennessee A & I is still the only college in the country to have a serious track program for women," she said.

In between Olympic games, Olga tried in her own way to combat the still prevailing myths about athletic women. "Many slim and attractive European girls have done extremely well against stronger and heavier women," she told her audiences of school girls and club women in her home town of Santa Monica, California.

Because she believed in practicing what she preached, Olga lost 30 of her 178 pounds. "I lost four inches from my southern pole, two inches from my waist and no inches where I didn't want to lose," she said. Her schedule called for a minimum of a half hour of hard exercise every day plus a careful diet. Whenever and wherever she could, she encouraged participation in the skill sports of the field —discus, javelin, jumping, and shot put.

Certainly women's participation in track and field needed encouragement. Running, jumping, throwing, and spearing may have been man's earliest pastimes. With little equipment needed and no rules to learn, individual competition among men dates back to the cavemen.

But alas, where were the females of the species? In the trees, in the caves, in the kitchens? Wherever they were, they did not appear on the Olympic cinder tracks until the 1928 games in Amsterdam, when 19 girls from America competed in a five-event program. Considering this nation's lack of emphasis on track sports, it was surprising that Elizabeth Robinson of Illinois won a gold medal in the 100-meter dash.

For the next 30 years, the United States produced only a handful of women gold medalists in Olympic track and field: Babe Didrikson (1932) and Helen Stephens (1936) in the sprints; Jean Shiley (1932), Alice Coachman (1948), and Mildred McDaniel (1956) in the high jump; Lillian Copeland (1932) in the discus; and Babe Didrikson (1932) in the javelin.

With the Rome Olympics in 1960, American women began to acquire a new look. They won six gold medals in running. Now, as Olga Connolly had hoped, there would also be greater interest and emphasis on the field events as well. By 1965, the 24 women's athletic clubs of ten years earlier had grown to 200.

By the 1968 Olympic games in Mexico City, America had produced a whole new crop of promising young athletes. Ollan Cassell, 1964 Olympic gold medalist in the 1600-meter relay who is track and field administrator for the AAU, observed, "There is a whole new breed of female athletes emerging in this country. They are young and pretty and beautiful to watch. What is more important, they are willing to train hard and are doing well in the technique sports. These girls have finally discovered that you don't have to weigh 300 pounds, or have bulging muscles to be a champion."

Who were these new athletes? Billee Pat Daniels Winslow was a tall, striking blonde from San Mateo, California. She was national champion in the long jump in 1967 and competed in the five-event pentathlon in the 1964 Olympics, when it was held for the first time. The pentathlon consists of a grueling competition in a 200-meter dash, shot put, high jump, long jump, and 80-meter hurdles. In

Wyomia Tyus, breasting the tape here in the 100-meter dash in the 1964 Olympics at Tokyo, won the same event in the 1968 Olympics at Mexico City.

the 1967 Pan-American games in Winnipeg, Canada, the glamorous Mrs. Winslow won the same event.

During the latter part of the fifties, the "new breed" athletes also competed in most of the other field events. Outstanding in the high jump was Eleanor Montgomery; in the discus, Carol Moeske; in the javelin RaNae Bair and Barbara Friedrich. Even in the shot put America was producing champions. Earlene Brown, Lynn Graham, and Maren Seidler were the leaders in an event usually associated with big-muscled men.

American women continued to show their superiority in the running events. The world records for 100 yards and 100 meters were set by Wyomia Tyus of Griffin, Georgia, in 1965, and in 1967 Barbara Ferrell also met the record time of 11.1 seconds for the 100-meter dash. Wyomia was America's gold medalist for the 100 meters in the 1964 and 1968 Olympics.

Running right along with Wyomia was Edith McGuire, who won the gold medal for the 200-meter dash. In 1967 she ran the 220 in 24.1 seconds, this time for a world record. Ed Temple, an Olympic track coach, once said that it would take three women to fill Wilma Rudolph's sneakers. He believed that Edith might be those three women. "She has the same loose gait," he said, "and the same ability to relax right up until the starting gun explodes."

In the longer, more grueling races, too, women were proving their abilities. On July 12, 1965, the AAU track and field championships included a 1500-meter race for women for the first time. It was won by a fifteen-year-old, straight-A student from Sacramento, California, Marie Mulder. At the 1967 AAU championship meet, Doris Brown set the world mark for the women's indoor mile at 4:43.3. This twenty-four-year-old housewife from Seattle, Washington, had run the mile in less than a minute more than the time set by the famed Jim Ryun, the world's fastest miler. Doris was also the 1967 AAU cross-country champion, again running in a race that had long been reserved for hardy males.

That same year, a beautiful, blonde social worker from

Washington, Charlotte Cooke, set the world indoor records for the 440- and 880-yard runs. And in the 1968 Olympics, another attractive American, Madeline Manning, ran off with the gold medal in the 800-meter race. This half-mile victory was additional proof that American women had the strength and endurance to train and compete in the long-distance races.

The annual Boston Marathon was another traditionally masculine bastion. But even its walls came down. One brisk day in April 1966, a hooded figure was seen among the 415 starters of the 26-mile course. When the race was over, the hood came off to unveil a twenty-three-year-old housewife. Although she was never officially entered in the race, Mrs. Roberta Gibb Bingay finished ahead of 290 men.

"I was just in it for the fun," she said. "I did want to make people see something different that would shake them up a little bit, and maybe change some old-fashioned attitudes."

And so, over hill and dale, faster and farther, the women of America run on—leaving tradition and myths behind.

CHAPTER 4

The
Racketeers

IN NEW YORK, London, Mexico City, Rome—in the large cities and some of the small ones all around the world—newspapers on the morning of September 11, 1967, carried stories echoing the headline, "And a King is Queen."

The King was twenty-three-year-old Mrs. Billie Jean King of Berkeley, California, who became queen by defeating England's Ann Haydon Jones in the United States Women's National Singles Tennis Championship at Forest Hills, New York. During this same tournament, Billie Jean won the women's doubles and mixed-doubles titles as well, a feat not accomplished since Doris Hart's victories in 1951.

Earlier that summer, in England, Mrs. King had taken a similar triple crown at Wimbledon. This spectacular triple triumph in both the British and American tournaments had not occurred since another American woman, Alice Marble, achieved the same in 1939.

Billie Jean King now stood indisputably at the top of international tennis. She had joined the ranks of such American greats as Helen Wills Moody, Helen Hull Jacobs, Alice Marble, Doris Hart, Maureen Connolly, and Althea Gibson.

As a youngster, however, Billie Jean Moffitt was an ace at softball, not tennis. Her father, an engineer with the Long Beach, California, fire department, considered baseball an unladylike sport. "So I convinced her she should try something else," he said. "I enrolled her in the city's free tennis training program and she did the rest."

When she was twelve, only a year after first picking up a tennis racket, Billie Jean won her first tournament. There was no stopping her after that. She played tennis every day during the summer and after school and on weekends. Neither Mr. or Mrs. Moffitt played tennis and Billie Jean's new-found love for the sport came as a surprise. "She just talked about wanting to be a champion. She said there wasn't anything more in the world she wanted than to play some day at Wimbledon," said her dad.

When she was sixteen, "Jillie Bean" as she was called, was ranked nineteenth in the country, which was quite an accomplishment for a youngster who had been playing only four years. At that point her training began in earnest. Her teacher was former Wimbledon and U.S. champion Alice Marble, who was a coach and tennis club owner in Palm Springs, California. Miss Marble invited Billie Jean to stay with her on weekends.

"She was so crazy about tennis, I'd have to lock her in her room to study," said the coach of her new pupil. When Billie Jean played tennis, however, she needed no encouragement to work. Miss Marble changed her whole game around, took it apart and put it back together again.

Poor Billie Jean was also put on a strict diet—no more ice cream, her favorite treat—and was kept in shape off the courts by running and skipping rope. All the hours of practice and self-discipline paid off. When Alice Marble finished with her, only six months later, Billie Jean's 1960 ranking had jumped from nineteenth to fourth!

Billie Jean King is on her way to victory against Britain's Ann Jones in the 1967 finals at Wimbledon, England.

In 1962 Billie Jean scored her first big victory at Wimbledon, when as a bouncy, bespectacled eighteen-year-old she defeated the favored top-ranking player, Australia's Margaret Smith, in the first round. Her British fans, who dubbed her "Little Miss Moffitt," were charmed by her. A delightful young lady, with an expressive face, Billie Jean was vivacious and talkative, and the crowds adored this. "The crowd helped me a great deal—if the underdog makes a point, everyone claps, and, boy you just go," she told reporters after the match.

Billie Jean's sense of humor made her one of the most popular players on the circuit. In 1965, when she married Larry King, a law student at the University of California at Berkeley, she quipped, "All that running and skipping was useful. I met Larry at California State College where I was studying, and he chased me till I caught him."

Larry sometimes plays with his wife in mixed doubles tournaments. If they lose, Billie Jean still maintains her good grace. "After all," she says, "you don't love a person for winning a game of tennis."

As with most newlyweds, Billie Jean found it hard to be away from Larry for the extended periods of time necessary on the tennis circuit. This, too, she learned to take with her usual good spirit. "Oh well, Larry and I seem to accomplish our separate goals better apart." With a burst of wifely pride she added, "He'll probably get all A's anyway while I'm away."

In April 1968, Billie Jean announced that she would turn professional. Her contract, as announced by the National Tennis League and Madison Square Garden, "was in the neighborhood of $40,000 to $50,000 and could increase to $70,000 through tournament victories." By the fall of 1971, Billie Jean had become the first woman athlete to earn $100,000 in a single year.

It is likely that many more Americans will get to see Mrs. King in professional competition. Her particular brand of tennis is a spectator's delight. She plays a hard, fierce, aggressive game. As one sports writer commented, "She buzzes the net like a torpedo approaching for the kill." She has impressed even the most skeptical of males,

Clark Graebner, a leading tennis player and member of the Davis Cup team. "Women's tennis is awful," he once remarked, "but I would walk from Cleveland to New York to watch Billie Jean play."

Women's tennis was not always a powerful and exciting game. When Mary Ewing Outerbridge brought lawn tennis to this country from Bermuda in 1874, it was considered a very ladylike, even sissyish sport. As one book of the period commented, "It is perhaps the only outdoor sport of an athletic character that invites skill of lady contestants and at the same time assures perfect conformity with the rules of propriety and etiquette."

It was so much the ladies' game that when women first appeared at the second modern Olympic games in Paris in 1900, six females took part in the only event open to women—lawn tennis.

Men showed little interest in the sport and the first tennis clubs were organized primarily for women, with an occasional man sneaking in just for the fun of it. Although tournaments were held earlier, it was not until 1887 that a national women's championship was established.

When Ellen F. Hensell became the first national tennis queen, she wore a long, heavily starched cotton skirt, nipped in at the waist by a black belt. Her arms were similarly hampered by a long-sleeved shirt, and around her neck she wore a man's black tie. It was hardly the type of costume that would encourage much running, reaching, or smashing. Lawn tennis was a boring base-line game admirably suited to the ladies of the time. The early champions—May Sutton, Elizabeth Moore, Hazel Hotchkiss, Mrs. George Wightman, and Mary Browne—all played in similar attire and it began to look as if women's tennis would be forever hampered.

Credit must be given to the men for finally giving this ladylike sport the impetus it needed to change. Once the men got on the courts (the first national championship for men was in 1881), it became apparent that tennis could be a game of strength, energy, and cunning. Although the costume still did not change much, the game did, and women began to develop new standards—deep volleys, good ground strokes, fast pick-ups, and backhand drives to the farthest ends of the court. Early champions of the new tennis had to discover these skills for themselves. There were no great coaches or past women champions who could show the way. So the women watched the men to find new techniques.

One such do-it-yourself player was Helen Wills, born in Centerville, California, in 1906. When she first saw the great tennis champion Billy Johnston lash out at the ball, she tried to imitate his power and accuracy. "I shall never forget my first forehand drive. I was a little girl with pigtails flying, playing on one of the side courts at the Berkeley Tennis Club. I didn't intend to drive, because I didn't know anything about strokes and their names. But when my ball went over the net, I knew that I had discovered a new and satisfying way of hitting the ball."

Before Miss Wills ended her career in 1938, she had discovered strokes so effective that her record is still hard to believe. She won the Wimbledon singles eight times, along with three doubles titles. She took seven U.S. singles titles, and four doubles crowns. She played in ten Wightman Cup matches, winning 18 out of 20 singles matches. She also became the only American woman to win an Olympic gold medal for singles play in tennis. All told, Helen Wills won the two most important titles in women's tennis, the U.S. Nationals and Wimbledon, more times than any other woman in history.

When Helen was a little girl, she decided to play tennis only because her best friend, a boy, liked the game better than anything else. Helen's father, a sports-loving doctor, played tennis and he encouraged his daughter by playing with her often. On her fourteenth birthday, when Helen beat him for the first time, he rewarded her with a membership in the Berkeley Tennis Club. There she won her first championship, the Pacific Coast Juniors. At fifteen she won the national junior girls title, and at sixteen she reached the U.S. finals at Forest Hills, only to be defeated by Molla Mallory, winner of the Nationals eight times.

The following year, 1923, in the brand new horseshoe stadium at Forest Hills, she defeated Mrs. Mallory to become the youngest woman to capture the crown since May Sutton in 1904.

Although Helen Wills will forever be remembered as America's greatest tennis queen, she was also a woman of remarkable versatility. She was a brilliant student who worked long hours on her studies and often just squeezed her tennis practice in between her classes and homework assignments. Her major was art and she exhibited such talent that when she wrote her autobiography, *Tennis,* in 1928, she did all of the illustrations herself.

When Helen graduated from college, her studiousness was appropriately rewarded. "I found that I had won a prize in my studies, which I shall cherish always more (I fear I must admit) than any of my tennis prizes—a Phi Beta Kappa key—and when they pinned it over my fast-beating heart, I experienced one of the happiest moments of my life."

Whatever Helen Wills did she did wholeheartedly and with such intense preoccupation that her determination showed on her face. Her nickname, Little Miss Poker Face, reflected this extreme concentration. "When I play," she said, "I become entirely absorbed in the game. I love the feel of hitting the ball hard, the pleasure of a rally. . . . Any one who really loves the game can hardly be blamed for becoming completely absorbed by it while in the fun of play."

Always the student, Helen developed a regimen during her tennis career which was based on common sense and devotion to healthy living. She passed this program on to women everywhere when she wrote her book. "Nine hours of sleep, no two late nights in succession, regular meals and a well-balanced diet with many fruits, vegetables and meats that build firm tissue."

Her practice schedule was consistent but never in excess. "Too much tennis tends to create boredom and the game should always continue to excite and stimulate."

Her tennis strategy was also the beginning of a new kind of tennis for women. "Aim for the all-round game.

This means good net and backcourt play, development of all strokes—backhand, forehand, etc. In other words the player should be at home wherever he may be on the court."

Yet Helen Wills and the women of her day were not always at home on the court. It obviously troubled young Helen to be ridiculously impeded by the long skirts, sleeves, and stockings, considered the only appropriate dress for women tennis players. She stripped for action on the courts by wearing sleeveless shirts, ballerina-length skirts, and finally no stockings at all. But this change in women's dress did not come about easily.

In 1927, when for the first time she showed up at a Queen's Club tournament in London without the acceptable long stockings, she created quite a sensation. Letters to the newspapers poured in from an irate public demanding that she be rebuked. Editorials debated the subject, "Should the authorities permit uncovered calves?" The matter was settled by the traditional majority, when more than half of the women entered in the tournament courageously appeared on the court bare-legged.

The following year, the first shorts appeared at Wimbledon without much fuss. Helen Wills had led the way. That year she wrote in her book, "Unquestionably the short-skirted, sleeveless dress and the sensible way of dressing on the court is responsible, almost more than anything else, for the great improvement that has been seen in the standard of present-day tennis for women."

American women owe much to Helen Wills Moody Roark. She left us with a new game of tennis, to be played in comfortable fashion. Moreover, she was a queen to Americans, to be worshipped and imitated for her very special qualities. She was beautiful for her wholesomeness (she did not drink or smoke), brilliant for her devotion to hard work, and talented because she was so born and worked to develop and perfect her talent. She was this country's answer to royalty, our queen, idolized by all who saw or read about her.

One such worshipper was a budding young tennis

player from San Diego, California. Twelve-year-old Maureen Connolly was playing in the Pacific Southwest championships when she met Helen Wills for the first time in 1947. Maureen's coach, Eleanor "Teach" Tennant, asked the fifty-three-year-old ex-champion what she thought of Maureen's game. "Maureen will become the national champion in four years and possibly the world's champion," Helen Wills said with certainty.

Maureen was overwhelmed by the prediction. She had only been playing tennis for two years and there were still times when she would rather be playing ball or riding a horse.

Maureen's mother too, had had other thoughts about what goals her daughter should pursue. An accomplished horsewoman, Mrs. Connolly had been disappointed that she had not become a concert pianist. She hoped that her daughter might fulfill this lost dream.

When Maureen was four, she had been given ballet lessons. But she was such a "ham" that her antics disturbed the rest of the class and she had to be withdrawn from the school.

After that, Maureen, who was fast developing into a tomboy, was given singing lessons. Her teacher tried to make a soprano out of her husky alto voice and once again the youngster met with failure. All the while, Mrs. Connolly tried vainly to interest her daughter in the piano, but as Maureen said, "The inoculation didn't take. I watched the clock constantly, eager for the moment when I could race out and play." And play she did, with the boys in the neighborhood, jumping, climbing, playing softball, and going horseback riding. Even though there were cement tennis courts next door to her house, Maureen hardly seemed destined to become a great tennis player.

One day, when she was nine years old, she stopped at the neighborhood courts long enough to watch two very fine male players smashing the ball back and forth. "Their rallies were long and hard, their serves blistering, the net play dashing," she wrote in her autobiography. "I stood entranced. Suddenly, every game I knew and loved

With her bare legs and bloomers showing, tennis queen Helen Wills championed the cause of freedom of dress on the courts.

Maureen "Little Mo" Connolly, who was the only tennis grand slam winner in history, was the world's youngest singles champion at age sixteen.

palled. The tennis virus raced through my blood. I made up my mind to become a tennis player."

Maureen now haunted the tennis courts. Her mother bought her first racket for $1.50 and the little girl was on her way. The pro at the courts, sensing Maureen's determination to learn, traded her services as a ballboy for his lessons. How hard she worked—three hours a day, five days a week. Her progress was remarkable and when she was twelve, Eleanor Tennant agreed to take her on as her pupil. "Teach" Tennant had coached such tennis stars as Alice Marble and Pauline Betz. Now it was Maureen's turn.

Miss Tennant believed that everything in her pupil's life had to be given up for tennis. "Teach" knew that Maureen had the makings of a champion. She felt that only through hard work, practice, and constant devotion to winning could Maureen make it to the top. Her rules were rigid and Maureen had to give up all the normal pursuits of an active teenager. There were no late hours or rich foods. There was little time for dancing, horseback riding, or listening to her favorite records.

"Tennis, to 'Teach,' was no game," said Maureen. "It was a battle, and no field marshal mapped the strategy more carefully. She was the field officer, I was the troops, and we went into action with deadly purpose and total concentration. If 'Teach' knew the enemy, she also knew me, and how close she might drive me to the breaking point in practice before easing the pressure."

But Maureen never broke. Spurred on by an overwhelming need to win, she tackled her opponents with almost a fierce hatred. "The tennis court became my secret jungle and I, a lonely, fear-stricken hunter. I was a strange little girl armed with hate, fear and a Golden Racket," she said.

When Maureen was fourteen, she played the tennis circuit for the first time. She won 56 straight tournaments, became the California junior champion, and before the year was out had become the youngest winner of the national junior championship.

In 1951, when she was sixteen, just four years after

Helen Wills had first watched her play, "Little Mo," as the world had come to know her, defeated Shirley Fry at Forest Hills in the U.S. women's singles to become the world's youngest champion. She won the championship two more consecutive times and each year was voted Woman Athlete of the Year by the Helms Foundation. In 1953, when Maureen was only nineteen, she became the first woman in history to win all the world's major tennis tournaments in one year—a "grand slam" record which still stands today.

Tragically, Little Mo's career ended abruptly. In 1954, she severely injured her leg in a horseback riding accident. Although she worked long and hard to make a comeback, the muscles in her calf were never the same again.

The following year, Maureen married Norman Brinker, a former member of the U.S. equestrian team. For the next 15 years, in addition to raising her two children, she devoted herself to teaching tennis to other youngsters. Maureen was happy with her new position and accepted her retirement from competition without bitterness. "I've had a full life with lots of travel and I've met so many wonderful people," she said. "Now I'm going to be a housewife. It's a new career and I'm awfully happy with it."

But even this career was cut short for the spunky champion. Early in 1969, after only 34 years of life, Little Mo died of cancer.

Maureen Connolly's reign had a profound effect on young athletes. She had proved to them the value of hard work and discipline. Tennis champs are made, not born, and a little freckle-faced girl only 63 inches tall has as much of a chance to glow in the sports arena as any strong, strapping male. Certainly age and size could no longer be considered an obstacle to a truly dedicated athlete.

But there were still other barriers to hurdle. On athletic fields everywhere, in all sports, another battle was yet to be waged. Although history books had recorded that the Negro in America had been freed in 1863 by the Emancipation Proclamation, this country's black athletes knew that this was not entirely true.

In 1927, when Althea Gibson was born in Silver, South Carolina, there were few blacks, male or female, who had achieved fame in the sports arena. The white community, still immature and bigoted in its attitudes, had made it virtually impossible for a black athlete to rise to glory.

Born into this type of society, a young Negro girl would have to have extraordinary strength of purpose, superior skill in sport, and a hardened ability to take insult and abuse, in order to reach the top.

Althea Gibson was such a girl. She was too young to remember her earliest years on a southern cotton farm, but her growing-up days on the slum streets of Harlem, New York City's black ghetto, were vividly implanted in her mind. These beginnings made Althea the fighter she was and gave her the compelling drive to find her place in the sun.

Life in the ghetto was hard. Althea lived with her mother and father in her Aunt Sally's apartment until her dad, a garage handyman, could save enough money to move his family to separate quarters. Aunt Sally sold boot-leg whisky in those prohibition days and Althea was exposed to alcohol, drunkenness, and a steady stream of disreputable liquor buyers very early in life.

Outside, on the city streets, Althea fought a constant battle with the neighborhood toughs. Her father, an admirer of professional women boxers (illegal today) taught her how to fight. As she put it in her autobiography, "In a tough neighborhood, where there is no way for a kid to prove himself except by playing games and fighting, you've got to establish a record for being able to look after yourself before they will leave you alone. ... I learned always to get in the first punch."

Althea hated school and played hooky all the time. "When I was little, the teachers used to try to change me; sometimes they would even spank me right in the classroom. But it didn't make any difference, I'd play hooky again the next day."

Althea Gibson (forecourt), the first black to play in the U.S. National Championships at Forest Hills, New York, opposes Louise Brough in August, 1950.

At home, in school, and on the streets, young Althea fought a constant battle for identity and survival. She knew she must find a way out of this jungle. "I always wanted to be somebody," she said in her book of the same name. "I was determined I was going to be somebody if it killed me."

But how? How could this black girl, defiant of authority, disinterested in school, wild and undisciplined, find her way out of the ghetto?

Her answer was sports. When Althea was nine years old, the block where she lived was converted into a play-street and closed off to traffic. For the next three summers, she played paddle tennis under the supervision of the Police Athletic League. Paddle tennis is a city game played on the streets with a rubber ball and wooden rackets that resemble large ping-pong paddles. It's a game that requires many of the same skills as regular tennis, and Althea discovered that she was very good at it. When she won the New York City paddle tennis championship in 1939, she realized that tennis held the answers for her.

Fortunately, there were others, too, who recognized Althea's potential and were willing to help. There was a recreation leader who believed in her, a tennis club that extended a free membership, a tennis pro who gave her free lessons, and a wealthy black doctor who took her into his home when she was nineteen while she continued her high school and college education under his encouragement. Dr. Hubert Eaton, Althea's sponsor, believed she had the makings of a great tennis player and offered to pay her expenses while she worked to improve her tennis skills.

In Wilmington, North Carolina, where Althea lived with the Eatons, she felt the bite of southern prejudice for the first time. "Colored in the Rear," "Whites Only," "No Blacks Allowed" appeared on signs everywhere. The Civil Rights Act of 1964 had not yet been passed and segregation was still a way of life down south. Unable to play on the public courts, she practiced daily on the Eaton's backyard tennis courts. When she had no partners she played against a Tom Stowe Stroke Developer—a robot machine that fired balls across the net at her.

Before long Althea was winning all the American Tennis Association tournaments. The ATA was the Negro tennis circuit and when Althea won their national women's championship in 1947, she felt she had gone as far as she could. No blacks had ever played on the white circuit and Althea Gibson did not think of herself as a crusader for civil rights.

But Dr. Eaton thought otherwise, and he posed to Althea the most important question of her life: "How would you like to play at Forest Hills?" Althea replied, "I'm ready, anytime they are."

Early in 1950, when she was twenty-three, Althea became the first black woman to play in the Eastern and National Indoor tournaments. But as the summer drew closer there was still no invitation to any of the grass court tournaments and, more importantly, no invitation to Forest Hills. It looked as if the United States Lawn Tennis Association was going to keep its doors barred. Then, in the July issue of *American Lawn Tennis* appeared a plea from Alice Marble. "I think it's time we faced a few facts," she wrote. "If Althea Gibson represents a challenge to the present crop of women players, it's only fair that they should meet that challenge on the courts. At this moment tennis is privileged to take its place among the pioneers for a true democracy, if it will accept that privilege."

Several weeks later, in mid-August, the USLTA met the challenge and Althea Gibson became the first of her race to play at Forest Hills. Although she did not win the championship, her very presence in the packed stadium was a stirring sight. Dave Eisenberg of the *New York Journal-American* wrote, "I have sat in on many dramatic moments in sports, but few were more thrilling than Miss Gibson's performance ... not because great tennis was played but because of the great try by this lonely and nervous Negro girl. ..."

But Althea did go on to play great tennis. In 1955 she toured Southeast Asia for the State Department with Karol Fageros (famed along with Gussie Moran for her ruffled panties), Ham Richardson and Bob Perry. She became a top-ranked international tennis player.

Two years later, Althea Gibson traveled to Wimbledon with high hopes. She reached the finals and in short order defeated Darlene Hard to become the world's champion. She also went on to win the U.S. Nationals that same year and again in 1958.

At Wimbledon, Althea Gibson, once a Harlem nobody, shook hands with the Queen of England and later framed her congratulatory letter from President Eisenhower. "I think I've got the main thing I've always wanted, which is to be somebody, to have identity. I'm Althea Gibson, the tennis champion," she said proudly.

Though Althea's triumph was a personal one, it was also a national triumph for believers in democracy. An editorial in the *London Evening Standard* eloquently summed it up:

More than the Negro people should benefit from Miss Gibson's victory in this delicate period of racial emphasis in world affairs. It further underlines the willingness of the British to take to their hearts those of any race, creed, or color. And it shows that somewhere in the great American dream there is a place for black as well as white, in this instance for a courageous and conscientious Harlem urchin.

CHAPTER 5

Figures
on
Ice

FEBRUARY 15, 1961 was a glorious, sunshiny day with not a cloud in the sky. Six hundred feet above the Brussels Airport a Sabena Boeing 707 jet was circling, awaiting its chance to land. At 10 A.M. the control tower signaled the hovering craft to give a taxiing plane time to clear the runway below.

In the air, 18 members of the United States figure skating team were eagerly anticipating the world championships in Prague. Hopes were high. In the group was sixteen-year-old Laurence Owen, who three days earlier had become the North American women's champion and was the most likely candidate for a medal at the world meet. Her sister and fellow skater, Maribel, and their mother, Mrs. Maribel Vinson-Owen, ex-champion and coach, peered out of the small round window and watched anxiously as the huge plane veered away from the airport—north, toward the small farming community of Berg, barely four miles away.

Suddenly the engines gave an unexpected roar, the plane tipped to a 70-degree angle and, like a bird skipping a beat, began to lose altitude. A few peasants in the cabbage field below looked up toward the erratic noise and watched in horror as the jet suddenly began to plunge earthward, spinning like a top and finally exploding into a mass of flaming, twisted metal.

No one had a chance. All 73 persons aboard and an ill-fated farmer below died instantly.

"Skating has received an incalculable setback," said Pierre Brunet, famed coach of retired skating queen, Carol Heiss. "Nothing short of a decade can make a champion skater. It's up to the fourteen- and fifteen-year-olds now."

Gone were the lovely young athletes filled with hope and promise. Gone, too, were three members of the Vinson-Owen skating family. *The New York Times* mourned the tragic event on its editorial page:

There is a special feeling of loss and grief over the young athletes—and at the death of Mrs. Maribel Vinson-Owen, former writer of women's sports for the New York Times. *Mrs. Owen and her two daughters and the other members of the U.S. figure skating team who perished were all skaters in the championship class.*

Laurence's praises had been sung by *Sports Illustrated* after she placed sixth in the 1960 Olympic games in Squaw Valley, California: "Her free-skating has an air, a style, an individuality which sets her apart from all the work done in recent years."

Laurence had her mother's drive and ability. After her success in the North American championships in 1961 she had been America's only hope for the 1964 Olympics.

Mother Maribel, born in 1911, was the daughter of the late Thomas Vinson, also an accomplished figure skater. When Maribel was three years old, she put on her first pair of double-runner skates. That year, 1914, Theresa Weld became America's first figure skating champion. She won the national championship five more times until 1928 when Maribel, then sixteen years old, took the crown away from her.

Maribel, a master at school figures, was a bold and daring skater. The slender, graceful girl won the national title eight more times and the pairs title six times. She attained international prominence in the 1932 Winter Olympics at Lake Placid, New York, when she came in third behind the reigning queen Sonja Henie. Maribel was also an all-around athlete, expert at swimming, tennis and sculling. After her retirement from competition, she continued to contribute to ice-skating by coaching and skating professionally.

In 1945, a ten-year-old with a straight blonde "Sir Galahad" haircut whizzed past Miss Vinson at the rink of the Skating Club of Boston. The youngster, Tenley Albright, had already passed her first figure test. In competitive figure skating there are 67 figures to be mastered, all based on the tracing and retracing of two- and three-lobed figure eights. All told, there are eight figure tests to be passed before a skater is eligible for major competition.

Young Tenley, like many other enthusiastic skaters, loved to free-skate, but had no real interest in the repetitive practice required to master the basic school figures, which count 60 percent in competition. Tenley's father, a successful Boston surgeon, asked Miss Vinson to give his daughter lessons. Maribel, along with Dr. Albright believed Tenley had the makings of a champion and hoped that with proper guidance and discipline, the young girl might earn a place on the 1952 Olympic team.

Tenley progressed on schedule. She won the Eastern sectional title for juveniles under twelve less than a year after a mild bout with polio. She followed it up with the national novice title when she was thirteen and the national junior title a year later. In 1952 Tenley achieved her first goal: she went to Oslo, Norway, as a member of the U.S. Olympic team. There she won a silver medal. Only one other American woman, Beatrix Loughran, had ever done as well in the Olympics. Tenley was on her way.

The following year she became the national senior champion and went to Davos, Switzerland, to compete for the world crown. This title had never been won by an

American woman, and Tenley was eager for the chance to change history.

Ice-skating, unlike most sports, requires absolute precision on the first try. There is no chance to cover up a mistake or take another shot or put on extra steam. There is one performance in school figures and one performance in free-skating. The outcome is based on the sharp eyes and subjective decision of nine judges.

Tenley breezed through her school figures. She began her free-skate with an impressive lead, and whirled across the ice in a coral-colored skating dress with queenly grace. As the last strains of "Offenbach's Fantasy" echoed through the ice arena, it became apparent that the world had a new champion, this time an American.

In the fall of 1953, the eighteen-year-old ice queen was admitted to Radcliffe College near Boston, Massachusetts. Her schedule that year put her on an exhausting treadmill. She was up at four in the morning to begin her day with two hours on the ice. Then came classes, study and ballet lessons. In 1954, while defending her world title in Oslo, Norway, the overworked Tenley suddenly fell on the ice—in the middle of a combination axel and double loop jump. It was a humiliating as well as disastrous experience. Tenley lost her crown.

Perhaps another girl with three national championships and a triple slam (U.S., world, and North American titles) to her credit might have given up to rest on these laurels. But not Tenley. She was determined to win back her crown, something no other woman skater had done before.

With an iron will, Tenley increased her practice schedule, rigidly enforced her diet and physical regimen, and prepared for a comeback at the Wiener Eislauf Verein Stadium in Vienna in 1955. Her coach, Maribel Vinson, described that week in Vienna:

She practiced on the uneven ice in sun, snow and even rain. As the two days progressed and Tenley's lead increased with each figure she skated, I was able to suggest that she try for a higher average mark on the next figure. It was a dangerous coaching trick for any but an iron-

nerved competitor. A sparkling free-skating perfor-
mance, this time without error of any kind, made her, by
the unanimous verdict of the nine judges, champion of
the world once more.

Tenley had come back. From there she went on to the
Winter Olympics in Cortina, Italy, in 1956, where she
became the first American woman to win a gold medal in
figure skating.

Tenley had climbed her mountain and soon was to as-
cend another. After completing college and Harvard
medical school, she became a successful surgeon. Today as
the wife of philologist, Tudor Gardiner, she manages her
home and busy practice with equal competence.

A complaint long registered to the United States Figure
Skating Association had been that figure skating was
primarily a sport for the wealthy. Mrs. Sonya Fuhrman
Allen, a former Swedish champion and mother of American champion Scott Allen, summed it up: "Figure skating
is a luxury sport. If you can't afford it, don't get in it. I have
seen many talented kids who couldn't get anywhere because they didn't have enough money."

Carol Heiss, runner-up to Tenley in the 1956 Olympics,
was a poor youngster, daughter of a struggling German-
born baker. Yet she had the kind of parents who were
willing to make the personal sacrifices required to make
her a champion.

Carol, her brother Bruce, and sister Nancy lived in a
modest house in Ozone Park, New York. When she was
five she got her first pair of skates and to everyone's
amazement, she skated off without any difficulty and in
perfect balance. Since there weren't any ice rinks near
the Heiss home, Carol's mother took her pigtailed daughter by subway to the Brooklyn Ice Palace. There, the sight
of the tiny darting youngster delighted everyone.

When she was six, Carol made her first public appearance in an amateur show put on by the Figure Skating
Club of Brooklyn. Her first teacher, Ingrid Lordahl, was
so impressed with the little girl's talent that she urged the

In a sparkling performance in February 1956, sixteen-year-old Carol Heiss defeated Olympic champion Tenley Albright to become world champion at Garmish, Germany.

Under the watchful eye of coach Maribel Vinson, Tenley Albright works out at Cortina, Italy, site of the 1956 Olympics where she became the first American woman to win a gold medal in figure skating.

Heisses to get her lessons from Pierre and Andree Brunet, instructors at the Skating Club of New York.

The Brunets would not take on any pupil who did not have unusual ability, nor anyone who was not prepared to devote long years in practice and competition. At the audition, Mr. and Mrs. Heiss, who realized how expensive a skating career would be, wanted to know just how far Carol could go. "In ten years," Pierre Brunet told them, "your daughter can be the best in the world." Carol and her parents accepted the challenge.

In the beginning, little Carol had lessons twice a week. To earn the extra money needed, Mrs. Heiss took on free-lance jobs as a fabric designer. Since she would not let Carol travel alone into New York, she took her drawing board with her and worked on the designs while waiting at the New York Skating Club.

Now, too, Nancy and Bruce began to show promise on the ice and their parents decided that the younger children should also have lessons. The three youngsters, known as "the golden kids," were a popular sight at the rink, working on routines together. Costs continued to mount. Coach Pierre suggested that Carol take piano lessons to improve her sense of rhythm and ballet lessons for development of her style and balance. More expenses.

Mr. and Mrs. Heiss worked hard, cutting corners in every way possible. For years they paid for all of the children's expensive lessons and skates from their limited income. Mrs. Heiss and the girls designed and sewed all the skating costumes themselves.

When she was ten, Carol began to show her championship qualities. She won the Middle Atlantic and national junior titles. Now Mr. Brunet, realizing the financial burden on the Heiss family, suggested that they pay only what they could afford for his lessons. Still the costly skates and transportation fares to competitive meets all over the country were a tremendous strain on the household.

Carol had difficulty keeping up with her school work. Traveling into New York every day for practice and lessons was too much for her. It was decided that she should go to the Professional Children's School in Manhattan, a public school attended by children who are in the performing arts. The school makes provisions for its pupils to continue their outside careers (with the odd hours of practice and performances) and still continue with their required schooling at whatever hours are convenient to them.

Carol worked doubly hard now. She knew how important it was to her parents that their struggles should be rewarded. In 1953, when she was only thirteen, Carol went to Davos, Switzerland, to compete in the world championships. This was the year that Tenley Albright became America's first world champion. Carol came in fourth.

Carol was to meet Tenley again six times in the next three years. And always she would be the runner-up. In the 1956 Winter Olympics at Cortina, Italy, sixteen-year-old Carol was the youngest girl ever to skate for the U.S. On one of Cortina's coldest days, the half-frozen teenager went down in defeat to Tenley Albright for the last time.

Two weeks later, Carol won the world crown in Garmisch, Germany, ending Tenley's reign. The hard-earned victory came none too soon. Shortly thereafter, Carol's mother died of cancer. Carol, who had promised Mrs. Heiss she would not give up amateur competition until she had won an Olympic gold medal, kept her word. At Squaw Valley, California, in 1960, she became America's second figure skating gold medalist.

John V. Lindsay, then a New York Congressman, made a speech in Washington. "It is refreshing," he said, "to have someone like Carol Heiss set such high standards of courage and strength for our youth to follow." Carol and her family had proven that even in figure skating, you needn't be wealthy to rise to the top.

After the tragic air crash in 1961, the United States Figure Skating Association recognized the need for financial aid to talented skaters. It set up a memorial fund to honor the memory of the team's dead. Proceeds were to be used to defray some of the travel expenses abroad for our most promising skaters. A scholarship fund was also established to lighten the load for skaters of limited income. The U.S. had to build a new team from scratch and the USFSA tried to help. Would it take a decade, as Pierre Brunet predicted, to make another champion?

Three years after the fateful crash, a petite, sixteen-year-old brunette was happily practicing on her "patch" at the Broadmore Skating Club in Colorado Springs. Peggy Fleming was so intensely working on her school figures that she didn't notice the rink was practically empty. She could swing out on the ice now and practice her free-skating without bumping into anybody. This was why her family had moved from Los Angeles—so she could live right near a skating rink and have lots of space to skate under the watchful eye of a respected coach, Carlo Fassi.

The Flemings, like the Heisses, were also a family of modest means. Mr. Fleming, who had been a pressman for the *San Francisco Chronicle,* moved his family to Colorado to spare his wife the long, daily freeway drive to Peggy's ice rink. His daughter was good and he knew it. Mrs. Fleming, an ex-newspaper reporter, agreed that Peggy should have every opportunity to become a champion.

Life in Colorado was healthy and full of outdoor activities. Peggy and her three sisters thrived in this setting. They swam, water-skied, played tennis and golf. In addition to ice-skating lessons, Mrs. Fleming tried to interest Peggy in the violin. "Although I loved the music, I hated to sit still, so I gave it up after a year," Peggy said.

But music continued to be an important part of Peggy's life. Mrs. Fleming, who had played in a family orchestra with her four brothers, exposed her daughter to music of all kinds. Peggy loved the classics and folk songs, as well as pop singers like Judy Collins and Julie Andrews. Her sense of rhythm, timing, and selection of background music for her free-skating performances reflected this interest. She once told her sister Maxine that if it wasn't for music she couldn't get along in this world.

It soon became apparent that Peggy had a special talent. She added ballet lessons to her schedule and her style began to mirror a ballerina's. She was light and graceful, and moved her head and arms like a dancer.

Peggy won the first of her five national championships in 1964 and then went to the Winter games in Innsbruck, Austria. "I was so bright-eyed and full of drive," she said. "It was the most exciting experience of my life. But, I think the competition was too intense. One morning I overslept and the girls I roomed with didn't even bother to wake me."

When she returned home, after placing sixth, her ego was quickly deflated. "What do you mean you didn't bring back a medal?" her classmates asked. "I was just crushed," said Peggy, "but I think I really grew up as a result."

As Peggy grew up, her skating continued to mature too. In Davos, Switzerland, in 1966, she won her first world championship, and after a victory tour of England, Austria, Germany, Russia, and France in the spring, she came home looking forward to the 1968 Olympics.

In between her rigorous training schedule, Peggy tried to relax by learning to cook and sew. She helped her mother sew many of her glamorous skating costumes. She became an avid cookbook reader and on Thanksgiving she proudly prepared the entire family dinner.

She also tried to keep up with her studies at Colorado College, but found it difficult. "I want to be an elementary school teacher one day," she said. "At the rate I'm going, maybe in about 20 years, I'll be able to finish."

In 1967 Peggy made a clean sweep on the ice, winning the North American, world and national titles. Now, she was ready for the Winter Olympics in Grenoble, France.

On Saturday, February 10, 1968, millions of people around the world were glued to their television sets. The marvels of the space age enabled the ABC-TV network to televise the Tenth Winter Olympics live via Early-Bird and Lani-Bird satellites to all parts of the globe. Forty cameras were feeding into 21 monitors at the TV control center.

In the huge stadium, *Stade de Glace,* Peggy nervously awaited her turn at the free-skating performance. In the days past, she had piled up an impressive, almost unbeat-

*Gold medalist Peggy Fleming is flanked by
Germany's Gabriele Seyfert on the left (second place)
and Czechoslovakia's Hana Maskova (third place)
after winning the figure skating event in the 1968
Winter Olympics at Grenoble, France.*

able 77.2 point lead in the school figures. At last, the slender 105-pound beauty, in a chartreuse chiffon dress, glided slowly onto the ice.

The powerful opening bars of Tschaikovsky's *Pathétique* signaled the start, and Peggy was off with two double loops and a double axel. Her skating was mature and full of depth. She floated across the ice like a prima ballerina—effortlessly, with inspired grace. After a minute or two, the music changed to the melodious *Romeo and Juliet* Overture—a spreadeagle here, a double axel there. Another change of music and mood, this time to Saint-Saën's opera, *Samson and Delilah.* Always smooth, always fluid, Peggy was pure dancer.

At last, the climax of her performance, the most difficult movement of all, a spreadeagle, double axel, spreadeagle. After a leap in the air from a backward-leaning spreadeagle position, followed by two-and-a-half spins, it was all over. Peggy Fleming had won her gold medal.

To this she soon added a third world championship, before announcing her retirement from amateur competition. She was besieged with extravagant offers to turn professional. In April 1968, she accepted an estimated $500,000 contract which called for her appearance in TV and ice show spectaculars.

Whatever her future, Peggy will always be remembered for having regained America's supremacy on the ice. In so doing, she had honored the memory of those eighteen young skaters, so tragically lost in a cold cabbage field in Belgium.

CHAPTER 6

The
Babe

IN 1950, THE Associated Press polled the nation's sports writers to determine the Woman Athlete of the Half-Century. There was little doubt as to the outcome. Babe Didrikson was chosen almost unanimously.

The noted author, Paul Gallico, went even further in his acclaim: "She was probably the most talented athlete, male or female, ever developed in our country. In all my years at the sports desk I never encountered any man who could play as many different games as well as the Babe."

Babe Didrikson had a spectacular career: as a basketball star, an Olympic gold medalist in track and field, and a national and international champion in amateur and professional golf. She also excelled in every other sport she tried and could probably have become a champion in any of them had she so chosen. She could swim, dive, play tennis, ride a horse, ice-skate, shoot billiards, bowl in the 200's, and pitch and belt a baseball.

If the Babe could play more games better than most

men, she could also sew, cook, type, and dance better than most women. Although she was often called the perpetual tomboy, Babe Didrikson was also a warm, outgoing woman with many feminine interests. "I was always determined to be a great athlete. But I was also interested in the woman's things around the house, like cooking and sewing and decorating. I loved all the pretty things," she said in her autobiography, *This Life I've Led.*

Both the rugged and the domestic qualities of the Babe were developed early, in the loving, close-knit circle of family life. She was born Mildred Ela Didrikson, sixth in a family of seven children. Mr. and Mrs. Didrikson were Norwegian immigrants who settled in Port Arthur, Texas, at the turn of the twentieth century. When Mildred was born in 1914, the family was still struggling to make a good life in America.

There was very little money for extras in the Didrikson household and perhaps that was why young Millie had little interest in dolls, fancy clothes, and other traditional girlish pleasures. With four brothers to contend with, family fun naturally consisted of sports and rough and tumble play. Mr. Didrikson was an avid sports fan, and if he could not afford elaborate sports equipment for his growing family, he could certainly encourage their activity and physical development. In the backyard he set up a gym with bars for jumping and hurdling. In the garage he fashioned a barbell from an old broom handle with flatirons on either end for weight lifting.

By the time Mildred was in grade school, the children in the neighborhood had nicknamed her Babe because she slammed home runs like the mighty Babe Ruth. She had a good throwing arm, too, and demonstrated her skill by hurling a baseball 296 feet. The female Babe Ruth ran and jumped and played, along with her brothers and their friends, in every game or adventure they could cook up. She was strong and wiry, yet full of grace. From her earliest days, she was a natural athlete.

But there wasn't always time for fun and games. When the family moved to Beaumont, Texas, Mr. Didrikson, who was a fine carpenter by trade, was forced to go to sea to make a living. His wife had to become a laundress to feed her brood and since there were no washing machines in those days, the children took turns scrubbing and rinsing and hanging the clothes out to dry. Millie was also responsible for ironing her brothers' khaki shirts and pants.

After school Babe worked in a potato gunnysack factory where she sewed up the seams on the burlap sacks faster than anyone else in the plant. Her skill on the sewing machine increased through the years and in high school she won a prize at the Texas State Fair for a blue silk dress with a pleated skirt that she had made.

Whatever job young Mildred tackled, she did good-naturedly and with a strong desire to do her best. This optimism and boundless energy were as strong a part of the Babe's nature as her exceptional ability as an athlete. By the time she was in her teens she knew where she most wanted to excel. She was already an expert seamstress, typed over 86 words a minute, and played a sweet harmonica, but it was to sports that she now turned her full attention.

"I knew exactly what I wanted to be when I grew up. My goal was to become the greatest athlete that ever lived," she said.

Actually, young Babe was quite small for her age when she entered Beaumont High School. Since she was barely over five feet tall and weighed less than 90 pounds, she was rejected when she tried out for the basketball team. Her disappointment did not lessen her ambition however. She spent long hours in the school gym practicing alone. She didn't have any sneakers then, so she played in her bare feet.

When she got home from school she worked on her jumping and hurdling by running across the backyards and leaping over the hedges between the houses. When she was a junior, she finally got her chance to join the basketball team.

The Babe became a sensation immediately. Though she was still small, she outran, outdribbled, and outshot everyone near her. The Texas newspapers were full of stories

The Babe, shown here with St. Louis Cardinal Burleigh Grimes, pitched in an exhibition baseball game against the Philadelphia Athletics in 1934.

Among her many achievements, Mildred "Babe" Didrikson won the gold medal with world javelin throw at the 1932 Olympics in Los Angeles.

Wearing her favorite "lucky" slacks, the Babe blasts out of a sand trap in the finals of the 1947 British Women's Amateur Championship to become the first American woman to win that crown.

about her amazing ability on the court. The stories came to the attention of Colonel M. J. McCombs, director of the women's athletic program at the Employers Casualty Company. Colonel McCombs was looking for a high scorer for his basketball team. Mildred was scoring as many as 30 points a game and the Colonel, after watching her play, induced her to join his team.

After finishing high school with a B-plus average, she took off for Dallas to work as a clerk-typist at Employers Casualty and to play basketball for the company after hours. During 1930, 1931 and 1932 she gained All-American recognition for her exceptional play. But 1932 was an Olympic year and the Babe had her heart set on a new goal. Although she had never even seen a track meet, she felt that she was good enough in jumping, running, and throwing to make the U.S. Olympic track team. Along with Colonel McCombs, she organized a women's track squad for Employers Casualty and she was ready for the first hurdle.

Ordinarily an athlete specialized in only one event in track and field, but when the Babe was asked what event would be hers she answered, "I'm going to do them all." In her team's first meet, against the Bowen Air Lines girls of Fort Worth, she entered all ten events and won eight of them: three weight throws, the shotput, discus, javelin, broad jump, high jump, 100-yard dash, and 200-yard dash.

Her instant success and natural ability did not keep the Babe from practicing. She donned her sneakers at every opportunity and ran everywhere—up and down the streets of Dallas. She practiced her steptiming for the jumping events and her arm swings for the throwing events. In the summer of 1932, after having spent the year setting records in the broad jump, baseball throw, and the 80-meter hurdles, she set out for the National Amateur Athletic Union championships in Chicago, which were also to be the tryouts for the U.S. Olympic team.

There were over 200 girls at the meet—some in squads of 20 or more, representing various schools and clubs from all over the country. They were competing for individual as well as team points. The Babe was the sole entry from Employers Casualty. For two-and-a-half hours she raced from event to event. In the shotput she defeated Rena McDonald with a throw of 39 feet 6¼ inches; she won the baseball throw for the third straight year, and she set world records for the javelin (139 feet 3 inches), 80-meter hurdles (11.9 seconds), and the high jump (tied with Jean Shiley at 5 feet 3 3⁄16 inches.)

Of the eight events she entered, she placed in seven and won five. Single-handedly, she scored 30 points, which won the championship for Employers Casualty. The second-place winner was the Illinois Women's Athletic Club with 22 points—and they had 22 girls competing for them. The Babe was now assured of a berth on the Olympic team. The girl who had never left Texas was on her way to Los Angeles, site of the 1932 Olympic games.

This time, she was only allowed to compete in three events. Eighteen-year-old Mildred Didrikson, still not much over five feet tall and weighing only 105 pounds, won two gold medals for her country, breaking her own world's record in both the javelin (143 feet 4 inches) and the 80-meter hurdles (11.7 seconds). She might have won the high jump too, but placed second to Jean Shiley because of a peculiarity in her style of jumping which voided her final record jump.

In the press box afterward, the famous sports writer, Grantland Rice, cheered up the disappointed heroine by inviting her to play golf with him at the Brentwood Country Club. Modest, unspoiled Babe was delighted with the idea, and although she had never played a complete round of golf before, she took up the challenge. In her first real game of golf, the amazing Babe drove an average of 250 yards and posted a score of 102. Granny Rice, who had watched all of the great golfers of his time, wrote that he'd never seen a woman who could hit a golf ball with such power.

Now the Babe's interest turned to golf and earning a living. After a childhood without luxuries, money was important to her. She wanted so much to repay her devoted parents. "Whenever I got extra money," she said, "it always meant that I'd be able to do more for my mother and dad. My brothers and sisters were the same way. We'd never forget what hard times Momma and Poppa had gone through to raise us seven Didrikson kids."

The nation was now clamoring to see the new athletic marvel. So the Babe took to the road. She played some basketball with the Babe Didrikson All-Americans, a professional team of three girls and six men. She played tennis with champion Vinnie Richards, pitched an inning for the St. Louis Cardinals in an exhibition game against the Philadelphia Athletics, and was the only girl on the House of David baseball team, all of whose members had beards.

For a while she also appeared in a vaudeville act at the Palace Theater in Chicago. She and performer George Libbey would trade a few jokes, sing a song or two and then the Babe would don her track shoes to demonstrate her athletic skills. A critic for the *Chicago Tribune* wrote of the act: "The Babe skims a hurdle, jumps a couple of times, drives imitation golf balls and runs on a treadmill. Mr. Libbey bemoans the fact that the limited scope of the stage forbids her showing more of her extraordinary prowess, such as heaving the discus, flinging the javelin or tossing a basketball. And Mildred ends her turn by playing a harmonica with no mean skill."

Although the Babe was enjoying herself in show business, she was still an athlete at heart. After two years out of competitive sports, she told her sister Nancy, "I don't want to make money this way. I want to live my life outdoors. I want to play golf."

She entered her first golf tournament—the Fort Worth Women's Invitation—in 1934 and became the medalist in the qualifying round with a score of 77. She was eliminated, however, in one of the early rounds and realized that she still had many strokes to learn if she was ever to become a golf champion. So much has been written about the Babe's natural athletic ability that too often her persistence, endurance, and devotion to practice have been passed over. When the Babe took aim at the Texas State women's championship, she worked for three and a half months toward this goal. In her autobiography she wrote of her preparation: "Weekends I put in twelve and sixteen hours a day. . . . During the working week I got up at the crack of dawn and practiced from 5:30 until 8:30."

The Babe was working again for Colonel McCombs and during lunch hour she would go to the Colonel's office and practice putting on the carpet and chipping balls into his leather chair. After work she went back to the golf course.

"I'd drill and drill on different kinds of shots. I'd hit balls until my hands were bloody and sore. I'd have tape all over my hands and blood all over the tape. Then after dark, I'd go to bed with the golf rule book."

She won that Texas tournament on April 27, 1935, but two days later she was ruled ineligible for amateur golf on the grounds that she was a professional. The Babe refused to quit entirely. She joined professional golfer Gene Sarazen for a series of exhibition matches and continued to live up to her reputation as an amazing athlete. She regularly drove shots 300 yards and once stroked a ball 346 yards!

In 1938, when she was twenty-three years old, she entered the Los Angeles Open, one of the regular tournaments on the professional circuit, and one in which women rarely competed. She was teamed up with C. Pardee Erdman, a Presbyterian minister, and George Zaharias, a noted wrestler. Although the gallery was particularly interested in this trio, they did not get to see much good golf. The Babe and George seemed more interested in each other than in the ball. In fact, before the year was out, the Babe and George were married.

Now, with a husband to take care of her financial needs, the Babe applied for reinstatement as an amateur. While she waited she took up tennis under the direction of the famed coach Eleanor Tennant. As usual Babe went all out and before long she was playing with the best. In one practice doubles match she paired off with Louise Brough to beat Pauline Betz and Margaret DuPont—all of whom went on to win national singles championships. Babe, too, might very well have become a national tennis champion but the United States Lawn Tennis Association also ruled her ineligible for amateur play.

Babe and George decided to go abroad. They took a slow trip to Australia, stopping at cities on the way where Babe gave golf exhibitions. An Australian golf writer wrote of Babe's impact: "What this magnificent specimen of athletic womanhood showed us was certainly impressive. The plain fact is that Miss Didrikson can hit a ball farther than all except a very few men."

On the way home George and Babe stopped in Honolulu for a belated honeymoon. They stayed for three weeks in a rented cottage by the sea. "We loafed on the beach," Babe wrote. "I tried out recipes for Hawaiian dishes. I also rented a sewing machine and ran up a half a dozen shirts for George with those short sleeves and fancy patterns."

Soon after returning to America, the Babe was finally reinstated as a golf amateur and in short order began piling up championship titles again. She won the American Women's Amateur (1946, 1950), the British Women's Amateur (1947, a first for an American), and the World Championship and National Open (1948). Over the 1946 and 1947 seasons, she set an all-time record by winning 19 straight golf championships!

At the height of her career in 1953, when she was only thirty-nine years old, Babe Didrikson discovered she had cancer. Her vast world of admirers responded with affection and encouragement. Letters, telegrams, and gifts poured in from everywhere as she recuperated from major surgery. With her golf clubs standing in the corner of the hospital room, the Babe could not stay down for long. Supported by her husband, she determinedly fought her way back to the golf circuit.

Just three and a half months after she was wheeled into the operating room, the Babe was back in action, playing at Tam O'Shanter in the All-American tournament. She placed fifteenth. Two days later, also at Tam O'Shanter, she competed for the world championship and came in third.

Though her performance was still not up to par, her

courage and perseverance were inspiring. Despite pain and fatigue, the Babe would not give up. "One reason that I don't retire," she said, "is that every time I get out and play well in a tournament it seems to encourage people with the same trouble I had."

For her dramatic return to golf, she was awarded the Ben Hogan Trophy for the Greatest Comeback of the Year.

The following year, 1954, the Babe regained her championship form. She won the U.S. Women's Open by 12 strokes and returned to Tam O'Shanter to win the All-American with a score of 294, only one stroke above her own 72-hole record for the course. After her victory, she told the world, "This will show people not to be afraid of cancer. I'll go on golfing for twenty years."

But she did not go on playing for even another year. Tragically, the cancer recurred. Babe Didrikson, a champion until the end, died on September 27, 1956. She will always be remembered for her optimism, honesty, warmth, and courage. She was not only America's greatest woman athlete, she was an even greater human being.

CHAPTER 7

Swingers
of the
Fairway

ON NOVEMBER 9, 1895, at the Meadow Brook Club in Hempstead, New York, 13 cumbersomely dressed women turned out for the first National Women's Amateur golf tournament. Significantly, this major golfing event was held only one month and six days after the inauguration of the men's national championship. For even then, golf was a socially accepted, fashionable sport for women.

Seeing a picture of those early lady golfers, today's players must certainly be amazed that these women were able to swing at the ball at all. For they were covered from head to toe in hampering clothes. A broad-brimmed hat was held in place by a pin or veil tucked under the chin, a starched blouse with long leg o'mutton sleeves was covered by a vest or jacket, a wide leather belt nipped in the waist with a heavy brass buckle, an ankle-length serge or tweed skirt was underskirted by at least one set of petticoats, and metal fastenings accented the heavy leather boots on their feet.

As might have been expected, the lady golfers had none of the versatility and power of the men. One sports writer describing their game said: "The women swing at the ball as though they were beating off purse-snatchers with an umbrella."

However, the emergence of Glenna Collett on the golf scene changed all that. In 1903, on the very day that George Collett was wheeling to a bicycling championship in France, his daughter Glenna was born in New Haven, Connecticut. Proud pappa George, in addition to being a champion cyclist, was also an expert bowler and handball player, and an excellent golfer.

When Glenna was six, the family moved to Providence, Rhode Island, where Mr. Collett joined the Metacomet Golf Club. Glenna, a tomboy reputed to have driven an automobile at the age of ten, was soon joining her dad in his visits to the club. She proved to be a natural on the course and when she was seventeen she entered major competition.

Glenna's career was unequalled in the annals of golf. She won the National Amateur golf championship a record of six times beginning in 1922 and was known as the Bobby Jones of women's golf. Champion Bobby said of Glenna: "It is especially a treat to watch Miss Collett. Her accuracy with the spoon and brassie [commonly used golf clubs] is to me the most important part of her well-rounded game. It is, of course, her way of absorbing to a great extent the disadvantage of length which any woman must suffer against the best males, but she does it, with little disadvantage to be noticed."

In 1935, five years after winning her fifth National title, Glenna, who had become Mrs. Edwin Vare, appeared at the Interlachen Country Club of Minneapolis. After a two-year retirement to bear two children, she was returning to compete for her sixth National crown.

It was a cold, rainy, miserable day. Still, an unprecedented 15,000 spectators turned out for the match. Glenna was up against some of the best young players of the time: Marian McDougal (twenty-one), Marian Miley (twenty-one), Betty Jameson (seventeen), and Patty Berg (seventeen). Thirty-two-year-old Mrs. Vare had to play the greatest golf of her career in order to recapture her crown, and she did.

Bernard Swanson, sports editor of the *Minneapolis Star,* paid her a glowing tribute. "It isn't everyone," he wrote, "who, playing in their fourteenth National championship, is still good enough to cope with the next generation. And fewer still could win."

When Glenna was asked after the match who had been her toughest opponent in the tournament, she answered, "By all means Patty Berg. In fact, quite a distance ahead of the rest, and they were all good."

Red-haired, freckle-faced Patricia Jane Berg started golfing when she was fourteen because her mother made her give up her favorite sport, playing football with the boys. That year, 1932, she collected three old brassies, three irons, and a putter from her dad and thumbed a ride to the nearby Minneapolis City tournament for her first competition. It took her 112 strokes to get around the 18 holes, but only six years later she returned to score a 70 on the same course from the men's tees.

By the time Patty was twenty, in 1938, she was considered the foremost women's golfer in the United States. She was selected as "Woman Athlete of the Year" by the Associated Press three times. As an amateur, Patty won 40 tournaments, was twice on the Curtis Cup team (with Glenna Collett), and in 1938 she won the National Amateur title at Wilmette, Illinois.

In 1940, pug-nosed Patty turned professional and started on the second phase of her extraordinary career. Patty is credited with having done more for women's professional golf than anyone else in the game. She organized the Women's Professional Golf Association in 1946 (changed to Ladies Professional Golf Association in 1949) and served as its chairman through 1952. Now a member of the Wilson Sporting Goods staff, she has conducted more clinics than any other male or female in the industry.

Still competing in 1968, Miss Berg had won over 41

professional tournaments including the first National Open in 1946, the Titleholders (women's Masters) seven times, the World Championship at Tam O'Shanter four times, and the Vare Trophy for the women's lowest scoring average three times. Patty, elected to the LPGA Hall of Fame in 1951, proved to America that women could make money playing golf. She was the leading money-winner of the LPGA three times, averaging over $16,000 in prize money each year.

Patty shot a 64 in the Richmond Open at Richmond, California, in 1952. This stood as the LPGA 18-hole scoring record for twelve years. In 1964, twenty-nine-year-old Mickey Wright of San Diego, California, broke that record with a score of 62 on the Hogan Park course in Midland, Texas.

When Mickey competed in her first Women's Open tournament ten years earlier, she was up against some of the finest golfers in the country, including the legendary Babe Didrikson and Golf Hall of Famer Louise Suggs.

Louise, known as the female Ben Hogan, had once defeated male champion Sam Snead in an open competition on a difficult par-three course in Florida. At the 1954 Open, Louise and the Babe were the only two American women to have won both the British and American Amateur crowns.

The Babe had already won the Open in 1948 and 1950. Even now, while winning the tournament for the third time, she watched in amazement as nineteen-year-old Mickey Wright swung her way around the course. "Gee whiz, get a load of that," Babe said to her husband George. "I didn't think anyone but the Babe could hit 'em like that. If I'm around five years from now, I'll have my hands full." Sadly, the incomparable Babe was not around that long. She died in 1956 and statuesque 5-foot 9-inch Mickey took her place as the "new Babe."

Mickey was already 5 feet 8 inches when she celebrated her eleventh birthday in 1946. Her dad gave her the first set of clubs as a present—a wood, two irons, and a putter —and Mickey promptly broke all four in the backyard her first day swinging at the ball. She played on a regulation course from then on.

At twelve, she was scoring 100; at thirteen, in the high 80's. At fourteen, Mickey won her first tournament, the Southern California Girl's Championship. The following year, at the Invitational Tournament at La Jolla, California, she made her first hole-in-one and won the event. Mickey rounded out her amateur career in 1954 by winning the All-American and world crowns. She then made the difficult decision to discontinue her studies at Stanford University in order to turn professional.

Mickey ushered in a new era in women's golf. She was to exemplify a whole breed of exciting personalities in the sport. The professional lady golfers finally began to draw large galleries to their tournaments. But it had been a tough road to travel. While the men were winning as much as $50,000 for a single tournament, the women were looked upon with skepticism. Their game was considered either "powder puff" in quality, or "Amazonian." The girls had to project not only superior golf, but also personality, good looks, and charm.

Mickey drew the crowds. She played tremendous golf, often outdistancing her rivals by as much as 50 yards off the tee. In 1961, she won the grand slam of women's golf: the Titleholders, the Open, and the LPGA Championship. She was named "Woman Athlete of the Year" in 1963 and 1964. For five consecutive years Mickey was leading money-winner on the tour, averaging over $26,000 annually in prize money. When the thirty-year-old champion decided to retire from the tournament trail to resume her studies at Southern Methodist University, everyone thought the tour would fall apart.

"People come out to see Mickey play even when she's ten shots behind," said Patty Berg. "They know she can still win. She increases the gate, and that is what determines prize money." Kathy Whitworth, Mickey's chief rival on the circuit, observed: "Suddenly the top is gone. Even if I do turn out to be number one, it won't taste the same. Everybody is going to say, 'Mickey Wright wasn't playing.'"

But Kathy was wrong. The galleries continued to grow. Kathy was ranked first and in 1965 she won eight championships. She won the Vare Trophy in 1969 for her low-scoring average of 72.61, and that same year she headed the list for all-time career earnings with a whopping $268,974.

Betsy Rawls, the oldest and perhaps wisest of the group (she was a Phi Beta Kappa from the University of Texas), was another drawing card. Betsy, who had won the Open four times, a record she shared with Mickey Wright, had been leading money-winner twice and was elected to the Hall of Fame in 1960.

Perhaps the most exciting personality of all, however, was 6-foot 3-inch Carol Mann, an effervescent blonde from Buffalo, New York. Lennie Wirtz, the women's tour director, said: "Once you meet her, you never forget her."

On a golf course at Englewood, New Jersey in 1913, these ladies played in long wool skirts and stockings, and stiffly starched shirts with ties.

Leading all-time Ladies' Professional Golf Association money-winner, Carol Mann, shows the style that earned her close to $50,000 in 1969.

Carol was self-conscious about her height, but she was the pace-setter among fashionable women golfers. She was one of the few women to wear culottes on the tour, and was always particularly careful to look as feminine as possible. "We should all try to look more ladylike on the course," she said. "Being thought of as anything but a woman absolutely frosts me." Carol won the Open in 1965 and continued to charm the galleries for the next four years. By 1969, Carol showed just how far the women had come. She established the money-winning record on the LPGA tour of $49,152.50, a figure which represented her competitive earnings for that one year.

Still it was the "new Babe," Mickey Wright, who returned to the circuit in 1968, who had gotten the girls off the tee and started them on the big-money trail. "Naturally, I am flattered at being compared to Babe Didrikson," she said, "but I really don't think this is quite proper. The Babe was in a class all by herself."

CHAPTER 8

On Olympian Slopes

PERT, PIGTAILED Gretchen Fraser waited tensely for the countdown to begin. In a few minutes she would be the first of 31 women skiers to rocket down the perilous Mt. Piz-Nair slope at the 1948 Winter Olympics in St. Moritz, Switzerland.

The phone at the starting gate rang, indicating that the slope below was all-clear. "Five, four, three, two, one," counted the starter, and then twenty-nine-year-old Gretchen poled off, down the treacherous course for the women's special slalom event.

Being first to go down the unblazed trail was a handicap and Gretchen concentrated on the terrain ahead. She would have to weave in and out of the series of colorfully flagged poles, called gates, which were planted in the snow. She would have to execute clean, sharp turns while traveling at estimated speeds of close to 60 miles an hour. She would have to avoid hidden bumps in the snow, patches of ice, and other variations in the mountain's surface.

In less than a minute, Gretchen had reached the bottom. It was a flawless run, but because she had skied it first, she had lost precious seconds by using caution to track the course. The winner of this event, however, would be determined by the combined time of two runs, so Gretchen climbed back up the hill and readied herself once more at the starting gate.

This time she knew the mountain and, throwing caution to the wind, cascaded down, zigging and zagging without hesitation. In perfect control, she swivel-hipped closely through the narrow gates and reached the bottom in the combined winning time of 117.2 seconds. Only four other skiers were within even 61 seconds of her time.

The gold medal was hers. Gretchen Fraser had become America's first gold medalist in skiing! Since 1924, when the Winter Olympics began, the Europeans had reigned supreme. Now an American was queen of the slopes.

Gretchen had been described by the foreign press as "an unknown from America." (Her last major victory had been in 1942 when she took the U.S. National Slalom Championship.) The day before winning her Olympic gold medal, the international crowd went wild when she won second place in the women's combined Alpine race, a grueling test of speed and skill which has since been discontinued. Now, after placing first in the slalom, Gretchen was shyly acknowledging the acclaim of fellow racers and spectators alike. "I had no idea I could do it," she said breathlessly. "My husband will be especially happy."

Although this was her first Olympic competition, Gretchen was not completely unknown to American skiers. In 1940, she had become the first winner of the Diamond Sun event, held at Mt. Baldy in Sun Valley, Idaho. She won the same race the next year and followed it with the national combined and downhill titles.

Skiing came naturally to Gretchen. Her mother, Norwegian by birth, was a ski enthusiast. After marrying William Kunigk of Tacoma, Washington, Mrs. Kunigk worked for the development of Mt. Rainier as a popular ski area and encouraged Americans to take up the sport.

Gretchen started to ski when she was sixteen and it could have been predicted that when she was ready for marriage she would choose another skier. Donald Fraser had been a member of the 1936 Olympic ski team, and in 1939 he and Gretchen were married.

That year the newlyweds were both selected for the Olympic team, but World War II caused the cancellation of the 1940 games. Don served four years in the Navy, while Gretchen, like so many other American women, had to build a life of her own alone.

She taught swimming, riding, and skiing to amputees in Army hospitals. She also took flying lessons, and after clocking 1500 hours of air time, Gretchen earned her single, multi-engine, seaplane, and instrument ratings. She became a member of the Ninety-Niners, an international women's flying organization.

When Donald returned from war, he and Gretchen set up a small gasoline and oil distributing company in Vancouver, Washington. Don was the driver and Gretchen the bookkeeper. As life became more certain and settled again, Don urged Gretchen to resume her skiing. Despite her lack of practice, the twenty-nine-year-old housewife was able to make the Olympic team, and consequently ski history for the U.S. in the 1948 games at St. Moritz.

After her Olympic triumph, Gretchen retired from competition. But her life was far from humdrum or ordinary. A friend, W. Averell Harriman, then Undersecretary of State, gave her one of his finely bred Labrador retrievers as a gift. Soon the Frasers became experts in the raising and training of field dogs. With their son Donald, Jr., they often went out into the Washington wilderness on hunting and fishing forays.

The adventurous couple also owned a small seaplane and their excursions expanded into long camping trips in the wilds of the Canadian lake region. One year, Gretchen and Don were invited by world traveler and news commentator Lowell Thomas to spend two weeks on the Juneau Ice Cap in Alaska for the filming of one of his TV "High Adventure" episodes. Mr. Thomas claimed that Gretchen was the first American woman to live on an ice cap.

Gretchen still hadn't entirely given up her involvement in Olympic skiing. At the 1952 Winter games in Oslo, Norway, she served as manager of the U.S. women's ski team. Gretchen was particularly impressed with the captain of the squad, nineteen-year-old Andrea Mead Lawrence.

Like Gretchen, Andy was married to an Olympic skier. She, too, had skiing in her blood and had literally grown up on skis. Skiing hadn't become popular in this country until the Winter games were held at Lake Placid, New York, in 1932. This was the year that Andrea was born in Rutland, Vermont. By the time she was four, she was schussing down the hill in her own backyard.

Andy's parents had established a ski area at Pico Peak, Vermont. Every year the family vacationed in Davos, Switzerland, not only to ski, but also to pick up tips for running their own ski area. In 1938, they brought back a well-known ski instructor, Carl Acker, to head the Pico Ski School. Andrea's lessons began in earnest.

By the time she was eleven, Andy was competing against adults. She took second in the Womens' Eastern Slalom Championship at Pico Peak in 1944. Two years later, while racing down the slope to help an injured skier, she broke her leg in the only ski accident of her career.

When she was fourteen, Andy qualified for the U.S. Olympic team at tryouts held at Sun Valley. In 1948 she went to St. Moritz as the youngest member ever to be on the U.S. Olympic ski team. Although she only finished eighth in the slalom, the Olympics enabled her to meet young Dave Lawrence, a handsome teammate from Dartmouth College in New Hampshire.

Dave didn't give adolescent Andy a tumble until the 1949 tryouts for the FIS *(Federation Internationale de Ski)* team in Whitefish, Montana. Coming down the slope in a practice run, Dave lost control and tumbled at An-

Andrea Mead barrels down the slalom course to win the second of two gold medals in the 1952 Winter Olympics at Oslo, Norway.

Schoolteacher Jean Saubert, a silver medalist in the 1964 Winter Games at Innsbruck, Austria, became a TV announcer of skiing events.

When Gretchen Fraser crossed the finish line in the slalom event at St. Moritz, Switzerland in 1948, she became America's first gold medalist in Olympic skiing.

drea's feet. "She gave me a kind of scornful look, and it infuriated me," he said. So love bloomed.

The National Ski Association offered Andy and Dave a trip to Europe for pre-Olympic competition and practice. Andy won everything in sight, including Dave, and they were married in Davos before returning to a Wyoming ranch for their honeymoon.

In 1952, Andy and Dave, who was chosen as an alternate on the men's team, left for the Winter games in Oslo. Andrea was an unusual competitor in at least one respect —she skied for fun and not necessarily to win. "I know it's the Olympics," she said. "Everybody wants to win, but honestly, I don't care. I just want to do my best." Dave respected his wife's philosophy. "I've learned never to wish her good luck on race day. It makes her mad. I just tell her to have fun."

On the day of the giant slalom, conditions were poor on the Norefjell course. The run was shortened to less than two-thirds of a mile because of lack of snow. Some 300 Norwegian soldiers had to shovel snow from the nearby gullies and ditches on to the bare spots on the mountain. Andrea was ready for the worst.

In a brilliant performance, however, she flew to victory before an audience that included such royalty as the princesses Ragnhild of Norway and Josephine-Charlotte of Belgium.

Three days later, in the special slalom race, Andy took a bad fall halfway down the hazardous Rodkleiva course. She finished the run, but it seemed unlikely that she could make up the valuable lost seconds her next time down. Determined to do her best anyway, Andrea shoved off with a hard, fast jump turn and continued the quick poled turns through the 49 gates of the 508-yard course. On the last lap, she crouched daringly low and hugged the mountain the rest of the way down—literally into the waiting arms of her husband.

"Total time," blared the loudspeakers, "two minutes, ten and six-tenths seconds." Andrea had won another gold medal, making her the only American skier to achieve such distinction. She had shown the world that although

America's men skiers couldn't bring home the medals, a woman could.

Eagerly following the newspaper accounts of Andy's triumphs was a teenager from Guilford, New Hampshire. Penny Pitou had learned to ski when she was five on barrel staves strapped to her tiny feet with wide rubber bands.

Now thirteen-year-old Penny was the only girl on the Laconia High School ski team. She had just gotten the bad news that she would not be able to compete in the state ski meet. The school board had decided that a girl's place was not on a ski team.

"I'm more at home with the boys than the girls," Penny argued. "I guess I've always been guttsy."

And indeed she was. Penny used to play tackle with the boys from the football team. In some respects, although the boys wouldn't admit it, she was tougher than they were.

Penny didn't have to ski with the boys. She set her sights on making the 1956 Olympic team. "I would bicycle 25 miles the first day, run two miles the second, climb a mountain the third," she said. "And then, I would start all over again."

When Penny was seventeen, she made the team and competed in the Winter games at Cortina, Italy. Although she failed to outski her European competitors, she was more determined than ever. "If someone asked me if I wanted a 300 SL Mercedes, or even a six-year college scholarship, I wouldn't have wanted either. To win in the Olympics was the only thing I wanted," she said.

So Penny went to Europe to correct her skiing faults, along with fellow skier Betsy Snite. "I couldn't even turn properly," she said, "and I wanted to ski with the best— the Austrians."

Penny took a job as a translator (she spoke German and French) in Anton Kastle's ski factory in Hohenems, Austria. After a year and a half of working, practicing, and competing, Penny had developed her sense of confidence as well as improved her technique. By the time the summer of 1959 rolled around, she was prepared for the challenge of the Olympics.

The 1960 Winter games were to be held in Squaw Valley, California. During the preceding summer, the girls' team, coached by Dave Lawrence, worked out at Aspen, Colorado. Their schedule was the same as for the men—low calorie diets, gymnastics, road work, and even weight lifting. It was an exhausting regimen requiring strength and endurance.

The women's downhill race at Squaw Valley was scheduled on an awesome mountain known as KT-22, an almost vertical drop of 1,814 feet followed by a run of nearly a mile. Three quarters of the way down was a nasty 90-degree turn known as "Airplane Corner." When Penny first saw the course she said, "The best thing to do is shut your eyes and shove off. Even the lift scares me to death. I think I'd be much happier being a normal girl in school right now."

Of course, Penny was no average girl and she had been working very hard for this moment. She would be skiing to win. "I want to be the best woman racer in the world. I'm going to memorize every bump, turn, and corner of the course. You've got to concentrate every second. There is always danger," she said.

The morning of the race, Penny tried not to worry. Her roommates, Betsy Snite and Linda Meyers, had to take sleeping pills the night before. "I tried not to think about the course," Penny said. "But when I got dressed my hands were shaking. It was even tough getting a piece of toast down."

At the top of KT-22, Penny awaited her turn in the downhill race. She busied herself working on the edges and bottoms of her skis. By now, word had reached the starting gate that Airplane Corner had claimed 14 fallen skiers. The waiting seemed interminable.

At last Penny's countdown began and in a matter of seconds she was off in a flurry of powder. It was all over in 1 minute 38.6 seconds. Penny got her medal—a silver one—coming in only one second behind Germany's Heidi Biebl. "Only power kept me up," she told reporters. "If it had been anything but the Olympics, I know I would have gone down too."

Several days later, Penny won another silver medal—this time in the giant slalom. And her friend, Betsy Snite, took a second place in the slalom. The American girls with their three medals won more prizes than the entrants of any other nation in the women's Alpine events.

Penny came home to cover-girl fame. Skiing was becoming a popular sport in America and pretty Penny appeared in TV commercials, magazine ads, and feature stories across the nation. She added glamour to a sport revolutionized by stretch pants, machine-made snow, and the birth of new areas for skiers from novice to expert.

Although her career as an amateur competitive skier was over, Penny remained in the sport that had brought her national and international attention. She married Austrian skier Egon Zimmerman and together they became directors of the ski school at New Hampshire's Gunstock and at other areas in the Northeast.

In 1964 at Innsbruck, Austria, a sixth-grade school teacher from Salt Lake City, Utah, won an Olympic silver medal in the women's giant slalom and a bronze in the slalom. Jean Saubert thus brought Uncle Sams's harvest of medals in Olympic skiing to a dozen—ten of which went to the women.

Jean came back to the ski picture in 1968 via television when she was one of the announcers for the Winter games at Grenoble, France. She was able to view with hope and enthusiasm the increasing number of promising U.S. skiers such as teenagers Judy Nagel, Kiki Cutter, and Marilyn Cochoran.

The women of America were really skiing now. They'd found a new challenge. They skied for adventure like Gretchen Fraser, and for fun like Andy Mead, and for love of competition like Penny Pitou. But whatever the motivation, the snow bunnies were multiplying.

CHAPTER 9

The Mermaids

POISED 33 FEET above the water on the high platform, she looked more like an aerial acrobat in trim circus tights than a diver. Running through her carefully placed three steps to the edge of the platform, twenty-one-year-old Mrs. Pat Keller McCormick bounded into the air before twisting her lithe body into a spectacular dive.

Momentarily the 5-foot 4-inch, 125-pound girl was hanging in the face-upward, horizontal position of the half gainer, with her head toward the board. At the peak of her lift, she rolled over in a half twist which put her in a "swan" position. Now on her stomach, she went into her "tuck"—grabbing her legs above the ankles and hugging her knees close to her breast, before revolving in a complete somersault. After another half somersault, she cleanly pierced the water of the Los Angeles Stadium pool.

While performing these acrobatics, Pat was clocked through the air at the rate of 68 miles per hour. Her dive, executed with such ease and precision, was rarely attempted by men and was no longer permitted in women's Olympic competition because of its obvious hazards. Pat was doing this dive just for practice because she was training for the 1952 Olympics.

With two long strokes, she reached the side of the pool, pulled herself up and over the edge, grabbed her towel, and hurried to the locker room. This September day in 1951 had been a particularly exhausting one. At 9 A.M. she had arrived at the pool for a 2½-hour drill on the high tower. At one o'clock, after lunch and a short nap, she had practiced her springboard dives. From 2:30 to 4:00 she was home doing her housework, shopping, and preparing dinner for her husband Glenn. Now at nearly 7:30, Pat had finally completed her last three-hour session.

Wearily, she pulled her wool sweater over her head. She was so tired that she made a mental note to see the club doctor the next day to make sure she was in good shape to continue her training—11 more months, 80 to 100 dives a day, six days a week, 2,200 climbs up the diving board ladder every month. She had to be in good shape.

After a thorough physical examination, Pat was relieved to find nothing seriously wrong. However, the doctor noted on his chart that Mrs. McCormick had a six-inch healed-over scalp wound, several prominent scars at the base of her spine, fresh lacerations of the feet and elbows, a once-cracked rib and broken finger, a loose jaw that threatened to pop from its hinges, and a number of ugly welts across her collarbones.

"I've seen worse casualty cases," he told Pat, "but only where a building caved in." Fortunately, these were all diving injuries of the past. All Pat needed now was a good rest and a supplementary dose of vitamins.

Who was this woman who subjected herself daily to the dangers of a sport like high diving? Pat McCormick was a U.S. champion. In 1950, she had become the first woman to sweep all three National Amateur Athletic Union's outdoor diving crowns. In 1951, she also won all the AAU indoor titles.

In 1920, when she was only twelve years old, Aileen Riggin became America's youngest Olympic title-holder by winning a gold medal for springboard diving.

Pat McCormick, diving gold medalist in the 1952 and 1956 Olympics, receives the Sullivan Memorial Trophy as this country's top amateur athlete of 1956.

As a toddler, Pat rode the breakers at Seal Beach near Santa Monica, California. She grew up fearless of the water. In her teens she spent all her spare time at Long Beach Lagoon and Muscle Beach, where she fast developed into an aerial acrobat, tossed in and out of the surf by the strong, young crowd of exuberant surfers. At fourteen she won her first diving trophy, the Long Beach One-Meter Gold Cup.

In 1952, after six years of strenuous, often dangerous competition, Pat was ready to make her Olympic debut in Helsinki, Finland. She proved to be the greatest diving queen the world had ever known. That year she won both diving events—springboard and platform—and four years later repeated her stellar performance in the Olympics at Melbourne, Australia. Her record has never been duplicated. For her achievements, Pat was awarded the Sullivan Memorial Trophy in 1956 as the nation's number one amateur athlete.

Ever since the 1920 games in Belgium, when Olympic diving first appeared as a women's event, the U.S. had held a monopoly on the diving championships by taking the three-meter springboard crown eight consecutive times and the ten-meter platform seven times.

Aileen Riggin, this country's first and youngest Olympic titleholder, was only twelve when she won the springboard competition in Antwerp in 1920. Along with another junior athlete, fourteen-year-old silver medalist Helen Wainwright, Aileen was not permitted to attend the victory ball celebration because she was considered too young for such evening festivities. Not to be fazed by the committee's strict ruling, the youngsters "borrowed" two evening gowns from the closet of a neighboring athlete's room. Dressed in their ill-fitting finery, they crashed the forbidden party and had a wonderful time incognito.

In the years following Aileen's success, American divers continued to rule the sport—women like Marjorie Gestring, Georgia Coleman, and Dorothy Poynton.

At the 1932 Olympics in Los Angeles, Katherine Rawls was the only American woman on both the swimming and diving teams. She took a silver medal in the springboard dive and went on to dominate the water scene in the United States through the 1930s. All told, the versatile Kathy captured 24 swimming championships as well as five diving titles. She and Gertrude Ederle were the first American women to be elected to the Swimming Hall of Fame in Fort Lauderdale, Florida.

In the 1964 Olympics, Leslie Bush of Bloomington, Indiana, prevented Germany's Ingrid Kramer from repeating Pat McCormick's remarkable twin win. Leslie took away Ingrid's gold medal in the platform dive. In Mexico City, four years later, Sue Gossick also defeated Ingrid when she captured the gold medal in the springboard event. America seemed destined to continue flying high off the boards.

In swimming too, American women ruled the waves. However, it had taken quite a while to get the U.S. girls in the water. They were not only fearful, but also bound by heavy clothes and society's restrictions. In 1829, a writer surveying the beaches of America observed: "Because of the tides, females are afraid to venture alone into the sea and prefer the assistance of a man." There is no doubt, too, that bathing suits of the time weighed down even the most courageous women. In Frank Leslie's *Illustrated Newspaper* there appeared this description of lady bathers: "Some wear bloomers, buckled nattily about the waists . . . some are wrapped in crimson Turkish dressing gowns, and flounder through the water like long-legged flamingoes. Others are in pantaloons and worn-out jackets."

During the 1920s, thanks to such crusaders as Australia's Annette Kellerman and America's Ethelda Bleibtry (first freestyle Olympic champion) and Gertrude Ederle, the suits had been peeled down to sleek, bare-legged styles better suited to competition. The long-stockinged, full-skirted days of dunking in the sea were gone.

The Women's Swimming Association of New York, founded by Charlotte Epstein in 1917, blossomed into one of the world's great swimming organizations. Claire Galligan and Charlotte Boyle, under the direction of L. de B. Handley, foremost swimming authority of his time and the club's coach, championed the new six-, eight- and ten-beat crawl. With it they won many championships and broke many records. The American crawl was here to stay.

All through the 1920s, known as the Golden Age of Swimming, the WSA produced champions. Club members captured 132 national senior championships in 193 competitions. In the 1920 Olympic games, American women won four out of five events; in 1924, they won six out of seven and in 1928, five out of seven.

Helene Madison, an eighteen-year-old six-footer from Seattle, Washington, was America's "Queen of the Waters" in 1932. She won three gold medals in the Los Angeles Olympics: the 100- and 400-meter freestyle and the 400-meter freestyle medley relay. Helene's fame was due largely to the fact that she set world marks in almost every freestyle event from 100 yards to one mile—15 of a possible 16 records.

Helene, considered the best freestyle swimmer of her time, never seemed to be trying. Her easy, happy-go-lucky style left her competitors far behind and the spectators gaping at her seemingly casual triumphs.

In the 1940s another star appeared on the water line. Born in 1926, Ann Curtis was only eleven when she became AAU girls freestyle champion. Ann was taught to swim by the Sisters at Ursuline Convent in Santa Rosa, California. She became a shining member of coach Charlie Sava's team at the Crystal Plunge pool in San Francisco. There she swam an average of three miles every day. Before she was seventeen she had won the national senior titles in the 440- and 880-yard freestyle.

Ann was an unusually versatile mermaid. In 1944 she became the third person to score a swimming "grand slam"—four national freestyle titles (four events) in one year. That year she was awarded the Sullivan Memorial Trophy, becoming the first swimmer and the first woman in any sport to be so honored.

By the time she left for the 1948 Olympic games in

London, she had won 25 national championships and set many records. True to form, Ann won two gold medals and a silver medal in the Olympics. The official Olympic record book hailed her anchor swim in the 400-meter relay as one of the outstanding individual achievements in the entire Olympiad.

Retiring from amateur swimming in 1949, Ann married college basketball star Gordon Cuneo. In 1958, by then the mother of four children, she started a swim club of her own where she devoted long hours to teaching others.

During the 1950s, the Americans slowed down and the Australians dominated the world of water. With the exception of Shelley Mann, who in the 1956 Olympics won the 100-meter butterfly (introduced for the first time) and was our first champion four-stroke medley swimmer, there were no bright hopes among the American women. The U.S. needed fresh, new swimming talent, and so a nationwide program was launched. Under the direction of the head coach of the Santa Clara Swim Club, George Haines, and Dr. Sammy Lee (two-time gold medalist in Olympic diving), the AAU embarked on its "age-group development program."

Concentrating on boys and girls from 8 to 17, local clubs were set up all over the country with emphasis on good coaching and frequent competition. It was hoped that by starting training early, the U.S. could regain its swimming superiority.

In the spring of 1955, a perky eleven-year-old from the Saratoga Swim Club of California tried out for Coach Haines' Santa Clara team. "She didn't show anything other than a kind of natural ability," Haines said later. "However, I gave her a schedule of workouts to do over the summer. In the fall, after a few weeks of practice, she began to show her great potential."

That pre-teen was Chris von Saltza, who at twelve years of age narrowly missed making the 1956 Olympic squad for the Melbourne games. During that year she kept working and improving. By the end of 1956, she was an established champion, winning local and national titles and breaking American records. There would be no missing the Olympics in 1960.

Chris' father, a San Francisco doctor, had been a swimming and football star in college. He was determined that his daughter's life would not be consumed by her Olympic goal. "We never talked about swimming at home," he said. "I considered it just one of Chris' activities. Big-time sports are good for children if they're handled correctly. Chris knows that swimming isn't everything. She'll always be interested in it, but she's interested in other things, too."

Indeed, despite a rigorous training program, blonde-haired Chris managed to lead a normal teenager's existence. When asked if there were any disadvantages for a pretty young girl in swimming competition, she answered, "Yes. The chlorine in the water makes my hair look green. But my training doesn't interfere with parties and things like that."

The "things like that" included being a straight-A student at Los Gatos High, a member of the student council, and secretary of her class. Her enthusiasm for sports led her to join the entertainment and rally committees. As a cheering member of the Whisker Club, she waved a pom-pom and yelled loudly at football games in her long orange stockings, black letterman sweater, and gray skirt.

Chris had the wonderful ability of getting the most out of her day. She was a master at organizing her time. Orrin Matheny, vice-principal at Los Gatos, praised Chris as an all-around girl. "She is an excellent student . . . in the top of her group. She's also modest and unassuming. We're proud of her swimming ability, of course. But it is because of her success as a student that we're so glad to have her."

In 1960, Chris, then sixteen, went to the Rome Olympic games. As a result of the age-group development program, the women's squad included 14 swimmers and three divers whose ages averaged only 16½ years. The Water Babies, as they were called, made a spectacular splash . . . with Chris leading the way.

She won three gold medals and a silver. The firsts were in the 400-meter freestyle (an Olympic record) and the

Chris von Saltza, winner of three gold medals and a silver in the 1960 Olympics at Rome, Italy, was one of the first champions of the U.S. age-group development program.

Her third Olympic gold medal safely tucked away, Debbie Meyer watches her closest rivals battle for runner-up in the 800-meter freestyle at Mexico City in 1968.

400-meter medley and freestyle relays. She narrowly missed a fourth gold medal when she came in second to the reigning Australian queen, Dawn Fraser, who swam the 100-meter freestyle 1.6 seconds faster than Chris.

All together, the amazing 1960 Water Babies won five gold medals and three silver in the nine events and set three world records. The Australians' streak had been broken and the Americans were in the swim again.

The U.S. continued to reign in the 1964 Olympics when the women won seven of a possible ten events. The leader this time was fifteen-year-old Sharon Stouder from Glendora, California. Like Chris, Sharon won three gold medals and a silver—setting a world record in the 100-meter butterfly. Sharon, who also lost to Dawn Fraser in the 100-meter freestyle by only one stroke, was the first American girl to break one minute in that event. Donna de Varona, who at thirteen had been the youngest member of the team in the 1960 Olympics, captured two gold medals, and Virginia Duenkel and Kathy Ferguson one apiece.

In 1967, another teenager began her rise to national and international fame. Debbie Meyer, fifteen, a short-cropped brunette from Sherman Chavoor's Arden Hills Swim Club in Sacramento, California, set world records in the 400-, 800-, and 1500-meter, as well as the 880-yard event. Bob Paul, a U.S. Olympic committee official, said she had the most beautiful stroke he had ever seen.

Debbie was named by *Tass,* the official Soviet news agency, as Sportswoman of the Year, after a poll of 13 news agencies in Europe, United States, and Asia. Two other young American swimmers were named in the poll —Claudia Kolb, world record-holder at 200- and 400-meters, and Catie Ball, world breaststroke champion. These young women were America's hopes for the 1968 Olympics at Mexico City.

And indeed, all that was expected of the Water Babies came to pass. Debbie Meyer became the first swimmer in history to capture three individual gold medals in a single Olympics. Before the year was over, she also held four world records and had become the fourth female winner of the coveted Sullivan Trophy.

The long list of medal winners and world record-holders among the teenagers astounded the swimming world: Jan Henne, Sharon Wickman, Sue Gossick, Sue Pederson, Kaye Hall, and Suzie Atwood, just to name a few.

"Americans," an Australian swimmer commented, "do so well because they swim for individual satisfaction and enjoyment. The rest of us are under pressure to kill ourselves for our country."

The Water Babies of America will come and go. Like Chris von Saltza, who went on to college and then the Peace Corps, they will find pleasures and satisfaction in many other things in life. But for one brief moment, when very young, they were the glittering stars in the Olympic waters.

CHAPTER 10

Merrily
They Bowl
Along

THE ENGRAVED INVITATION came from the White House to the cabinet wives. The First Lady, Mrs. Lyndon B. Johnson, was having a birthday celebration on March 1, 1966, for fifty-four-year-old Muriel Humphrey, wife of the Vice-President.

"Dress accordingly," the women were instructed, for the afternoon's activities were to include bowling on the private lanes in the executive office building across the street from the White House.

Although bowling is a sport that dates back to the Egyptians in 5200 B.C., such a party would have been unheard of in America even 50 years ago. At that time, the bowling alley was considered a disreputable place for ladies. Women bowled at the risk of their reputations, most often in dark, secluded basements, behind heavy concealing drapes. It was as difficult to get women out to the alleys as it was to find husbands who would allow their wives to bowl.

In 1916 the first women's bowling organization was formed. The Women's International Bowling Congress (WIBC) was started for the purpose of providing and enforcing rules and regulations governing the manner of play in local leagues and also to sponsor an annual tournament. At its inception there were only 40 members. At the WIBC's fiftieth jubilee celebration in 1966, there were 2,821,747 women on its rolls.

One of the earliest and most honored women bowlers, one who dared to venture out onto the "dark alleys," was Floretta McCutcheon. She was born in 1888 in Ottumwa, Iowa. Floretta didn't pick up a bowling ball until 35 years later, when she was a housewife in Pueblo, Colorado.

Floretta had turned prematurely gray and was bothered by her plump, matronly appearance. Perhaps, she thought, if she lost some weight she could regain her youthful looks. A friend suggested bowling as a good form of exercise.

The first time she lifted the 16-pound ball, Floretta was ready to quit. It took a lot of persistence to finish the game with an unimpressive score of 69. For the next few years Floretta kept at it. Although she never lost her motherly appearance, her game took on the quality of youth.

In 1926, Jimmy Smith, the world champion bowler and national match champion for eight years, came to Pueblo for an exhibition game. Floretta, by this time the best bowler of her community, watched Jimmy's technique carefully.

"I'd been a self-taught bowler," she said, "because there were no instructors in those days. I tried to alter my style to fit his."

Jimmy returned to Pueblo a year later. This time the owner of the bowling alley took him aside. "Want to meet one of our local players?" he asked. "Glad to, where is he?" Jimmy parried. "She," replied the proprietor, pointing to Floretta.

The confrontation became bowling history. Jimmy rolled three strong games for a total of 687 points. Floretta's three games totaled 704. It was the highest series ever bowled against champion Jimmy Smith and he shamefacedly admitted that the thirty-nine-year-old housewife was one of the greatest bowlers he had ever met.

Jimmy's manager Carl Cain, recognizing the value of a woman bowler, offered to organize an exhibition and teaching tour for Floretta. Anxious to raise money to send her daughter Barbara through the University of Colorado, Floretta accepted.

Mr. Cain had a difficult time booking Mrs. McCutcheon as an instructress. "The proprietors would like the exhibition part of it," he said, "because a woman bowler was still a novelty. But they didn't think the public would take instruction from a woman."

As a counter-measure, Mr. Cain sold the idea of a "Mrs. McCutcheon School of Bowling" to newspaper sponsors all over the country. "I got the inspiration from a Cincinnati cooking school," Carl said. The results were beyond expectation. Once-skeptical proprietors now asked for Floretta as a teacher as well as a performer. Women who had long shunned the alleys came for instructions.

"Bowling operators told me they would have gone out of business during the depression's financial slump," Floretta said, "if it had not been for my bowling school. The great value of women to the bowling industry was that they generally weren't satisfied till they brought friends, families and clubs to bowl with them."

Floretta's tours lasted over a decade—until 1939—during which time she piled up an impressive list of records. Many of them do not appear in official record books because they were scored in either instructional exhibitions or in unsanctioned match play. All of them, however, have been accepted as a part of bowling history.

In one series of exhibitions, Floretta averaged 248 for 12 games. She bowled a three-game record high of 832 in 1931. She recorded ten perfect 300 games and nine at 299. Her ten-year average in over 8,000 games was 201, with a 206 average during the 1938–39 season.

Floretta, however, was not just a great bowler; she was equally acclaimed as an organizer and instructress. Wherever she went she set up bowling leagues and bowling schools. "Mrs. Mac," as she was called, was a warm, sin-

Girls and women of all ages bowl today with freedom and respectability, like this grandma and champion, Marion Ladewig.

A player on the Cleveland women's bowling team in 1917 shows the form and manner of dress of the lady bowlers on the "dark alleys" of the past.

cere woman ... silver-haired and stocky ... who looked more like she had just stepped out of the kitchen than a bowling lane. Women had faith in her. If she could do it, why not they? Floretta, the Pied Piper of women's bowling, was credited with having taught over 250,000 women and children from the ages of eight to eighty.

When Floretta died in 1966 at the age of 78, Mrs. Juanita Rich of Los Angeles, an official of the Women's Bowling Association, said: "I don't think anybody will ever set records like Mrs. McCutcheon did. And she bowled under such adverse conditions ... when 'alleys' really were 'alleys'."

At the time Mrs. Mac died, another great lady of bowling was prominent in the sports pages. Marion Ladewig, however, had a bowling career very different from that of Floretta McCutcheon. Mrs. Ladewig rolled her records during the bowling boom, the rise of TV, and the era of big money prizes. She was the queen of the modern lanes.

Bowling's modern times began in the 1950s, when AMF (American Machine & Foundry Co.) and the Brunswick Corporation replaced pin boys with automatic machines for setting up the pins. Palatial bowling halls sprung up across the country. The new establishments included baby-sitting facilities and restaurants, and were air-conditioned in summer and comfortable in winter. With machines to reset the pins, the lanes could be kept open around the clock, accommodating day and nighttime workers as well as housewives looking for recreation.

Bowling had finally become a popular, socially acceptable sport for ladies. The word "alley" was stricken from common usage, for it still contained the "dark alley" image of the past. The bowling lane had become respectable and its inviting doors opened to women everywhere.

In addition to the WIBC, the Professional Woman Bowlers Association, the American Junior Bowling Congress and the Youth Bowling Association were founded to bring women and children of all ages into organized bowling. They came from every background and economic level to find pleasure in this newly popularized year-round recreation.

Modern bowlers ranged in age from pre-schoolers to old-timers such as ninety-year-old Mrs. Sarah Kuckler, who bowled in a WIBC tournament in 1966. They bowled in leagues . . . as members of club, church, friendship and family groups. They bowled in school-sponsored programs. The boom of rolling balls and falling pins was heard throughout the land.

Queen Marion Ladewig spelled her first name with an "O" like a boy because her mother had wanted a boy. But Marion was far from being boyish in manner or appearance. For as long as she was in the public eye, she appeared on the lanes slim, chic, and carefully coiffured. It was not unusual to hear whistles along with the applause as the 5-foot 4-inch, 124-pound blonde added championship upon championship.

The glamorous Mrs. Ladewig was the first woman to win the BPAA (Bowling Proprietors Association of America) Women's All-Star title in 1949. She won it again in 1950, and when she returned to the eight-day tournament the following year, Marion put on one of the most outstanding performances in the sport's history. For two days she struggled in second place before zooming ahead to victory. She rolled consecutive games of 255 and 279, a two-game All-Star record which still stands. Her astonishing average at the end of the eight days was 247.5—a score which topped everyone in the tournament including 160 men.

In the years that followed, Marion won the All-Star event an unprecedented total of eight times. She won the World Invitational crown five times, the National Doubles twice, and the Women's International Bowling Congress All-Events title twice. The Bowling Writers Association of America chose her "Woman Bowler of the Year" nine times.

In the 1963 Associated Press "Woman Athlete of the Year" poll, she was ranked third after golfer Mickey Wright and tennis champion Maria Bueno. Although stars of swimming, tennis, golf, and track had all produced "athletes of the year," this marked the first time a bowler came even close to this designation. Marion Ladewig had made bowling a recognized sport.

In November 1965, Marion stepped up to the line in a Chicago bowling establishment. She took careful aim and rolled her last ball in the World Invitational Tournament. Cheers and clapping echoed through the hall, for those who were fortunate enough to be there were witnessing the fifth and final tournament victory of the amazing Mrs. Ladewig. Several weeks later, Marion, now a trim and attractive grandmother of five, announced her retirement from tournament competition.

She was half a century old. She had dominated the bowling scene for nearly 20 years, winning virtually every major bowling title during that time. Her man-sized average over those years was 190.

At the height of her career, Mrs. Ladewig was earning over $25,000 a year from bowling. She was commanding $150 a day for exhibitions, was writing a syndicated "tips" column, acting as a consultant in sportswear design, winning grand prizes in tournaments, and acting on the advisory staff of the Brunswick Corporation.

It was a far cry from the days when she earned $2.50 a day for sweeping up and emptying ashtrays at Morrissey's Fanatorium Lanes in Grand Rapids, Michigan. Grandma Marion exemplified the new era in bowling, a sport for young and old, bringing not only health and recreation to millions, but for some special few, prosperity, as well.

One of Marion's opponents was a tiny 4-foot 11-inch brunette from Philadelphia, Pennsylvania. When Sylvia Wene was eighteen in 1946, she went bowling for the first time, with her brother and sister. They made her sit on the sidelines because they thought she was too small to pick up the ball.

"I wasn't good at the start," Sylvia said. "It really took me some time to hit 100."

Sylvia, the daughter of a grocer, worked for her father in his store. In the evening, after work, she would go down to the bowling lane to relax. She grew to love the sport.

By the time she was twenty, she was running the family grocery by day and bowling every night.

"Teeny Wene," who hadn't grown at all since she rolled her first ball, developed into a gigantic bowler. In 1955 and again in 1960, she took the BPAA All-Star championship away from eight-time winner Marion Ladewig. She won the WIBC Highest Women's Average award for her 206 score in three consecutive years. In 1955, she was voted Woman Bowler of the Year.

Throughout her career, Sylvia was runner-up to Grandma Ladewig many times. When she defeated the forty-five-year-old champion in the 1960 All-Star Tournament, the headlines hailed Sylvia's youth. She was thirty years old then, and in any other sport she would have been considered old. That championship also brought Sylvia the largest purse in women's bowling—$5,000.

Teeny Wene's greatest bowling accomplishment was in achieving a perfect score of 300 three times. No woman had ever achieved this more than once in officially sanctioned play. When she rolled 12 consecutive strikes in 1951 in a WIBC East Coast League game, she was the first woman in that league to do so.

Sylvia Wene Martin, now a member of the AMF Bowling promotion staff, had showed little women all over America that size was no factor in championship bowling, just as Marion Ladewig had showed them that age didn't matter either.

Epilogue

The women of America have come a long way from the days of billowing bloomers and stiffly starched blouses. Though modern fashions may be faintly reminiscent of days gone by, sportswear will never again be restrictive. Yet women are still fighting to free themselves from the restrictions of a male-dominated society. The "lib" banner is flying strongly over such arenas as politics, family life, and job opportunity.

In the field of sports, too, today's headlines show women are continuing to assault the strongholds of previously all-male pursuits. A woman was the promoter of the Floyd Patterson-Jerry Quarry heavyweight match. Women have been given professional football and baseball try-outs. And a fifteen-year-old American girl is training for a career in ice hockey at the Kingston Memorial Centre's annual hockey school in Ontario, Canada.

In the Olympic games, the gals are now able to shoot

it out with the men on the rifle range in mixed competition.

Even the high schools and colleges reflect the influence of the women's liberation movement on the playing fields. A girl received a tennis scholarship from Tulane University. The New York State Education Department ruled that high school girls would be allowed to participate with boys in such non-combat sports as swimming, golf, tennis, bowling, and riflery.

The champions of yesterday played for fun, adventure, and competition. Today's champions play for all these reasons and for money as well. They have made a way of life for themselves and for the millions of women who choose to follow them.

ABOUT THE AUTHOR

A graduate of the University of Michigan, and an avid outdoorswoman, Phyllis Hollander is senior editor of Associated Features, Inc., packagers of sports books. Her writing credits include chapters in STRANGE BUT TRUE FOOTBALL STORIES and THEY DARED TO LEAD, which she co-edited with her sportswriter husband Zander Hollander.

The Hollanders live with their son and daughter in Baldwin, New York.